FARMER GOD

GOD'S LESSONS FROM THE FARM

CHERYL J. HARRIS

10 9 8 7 6 5 4 3 2 1
Library of Congress Cataloging-in-Publication Data is available.
ISBN 979-8-88738-834-2
ISBN 979-8-88738-835-9 (ebook)

To my childhood friend, Patty Campbell: There are so many more stories to tell, but your story and your willingness to let me tell it over and over again was the beginning of this work. Thank you for being loyal and a little bit naïve. Thank you for all the encouragement and support over so many years. You are not just a childhood friend, but a friend for eternity.

To my husband, Harlan Harris: I've never met someone with so many gifts and talents, yet you have consistently encouraged me in mine. Best husband, best dad, and best editor. I'm so blessed that your eyes read these stories first.

To my daughters, Cheylan and Taryn: You come from a long line of storytellers. I pray every day you hear God's Word in your heart and His story in your lives. I'm so proud of the amazing women you've become. You are both such a blessing.

ENDORSEMENTS

"Cheryl Harris engages her readers with stories that are funny, enlightening, and filled with life and leadership principles. Get ready for the unexpected when you read *Farmer God* because one minute you are fully engaged in the story and even laughing out loud when suddenly a biblical principle jumps off the page. Add this book to your spiritual and leadership formation library with a readiness for personal transformation!"

Dr. Marion Ingegneri

"Pastor and author Dave Rhodes has observed that while everyone has experienced their story, few people have interpreted their story, and even fewer can articulate their story in a way that helps them find their place in God's story. My friend Cheryl has and continues to excel in all three of these spaces as it pertains to her story.

My prayer is that all who join Cheryl for a literary visit to the farm find the courage to dig in their own soil and churn up the story *Farmer God* is sowing in their own lives."

Chris Peppler,
Lead Pastor, South Everett Foursquare Church

Important insights into true spirituality with the help of our barnyard friends. A helpful, memorable and impactful read for those who seek a meaningful, trusting and growing relationship with The Lord Jesus. I recommend this creative read to you!

Dr. Jim Hayford Sr.

We read the manuscript and loved it! Cheryl is a great story teller.

Every story was fresh, clear, funny and filled with life lessons.

We're hooked. We want more.

Dr. Richard Casteel & Reverend Becky Casteel
Casteel Ministries

ACKNOWLEDGMENTS

The famous phrase "It takes a Village" definitely applies to the writing and publishing of a book. The amazing folks at Trilogy Christian Publishing were amazing, encouraging, and of course, reminding! To this crew, I thank you!

- Shelbi Chandlee, Acquisitions Executive – Thank you for seeing something in this work and driving me to the final draft.

- Rachel Hiatt, Production Manager – Thank you for keeping track of all the details of getting started and patiently educating me in the next steps.

- Rhonda Webb, Project Manager – As a fellow PM, I must have driven you crazy, but I so appreciate your tenacity and friendly reminders.

- Grace, Editor – You were fantastic. You not only corrected some errors, but I appreciated your comments and responses, especially the funny quips!

- Cover Crew – How funny you are! You captured the feel of the book perfectly!

I also want to acknowledge the first editor on this project, my husband, Harlan Harris. With an eye for details and the importance of story, you read and reread the stories over and over again, asking questions of clarification and word choice. The submitted draft was so much better than the original draft because of you.

And finally, to the crew of travelers on our trip to Israel and Jordon, thank you for listening to me read my stories as we waited for our next plane at the airport. Your words and reactions were so encouraging and I am so grateful for you all.

PREFACE

So much of the lessons from Scripture come through story, and more specifically, agricultural story. Jesus walks through a vineyard and starts teaching the disciples about Vine and Branches. When He attempts to describe the Kingdom of God, Heaven, or a multitude of other spiritual concepts, He tells a story to which His audience can relate.

And not just Jesus. I have often referred to the Apostle Paul as the Great Contextualizer. Through his vocabulary, you can almost visualize his surroundings. Chained between two Roman guards, he utilizes military terms when writing to the Church in Philippi. To the people of Rome, he is at his most Roman. Regardless of situation or location, Paul knew how to leverage his own experience to make it more easily understood by his readers. Different methods, same Gospel.

Many years ago, while reading the Chronological Bible every day for a year, and with the prompting of the Holy Spirit, I started to write stories. I had never spent much time writing in the past and, frankly, had little expectation that anyone other than myself would read it.

As I wrote, God began to reveal Himself in those stories and experiences. I began to see Him, His hand, and His presence in those events where I had not noticed them before. In every writing, God began to show me spiritual truths on the farm where I grew up. In every experience, it was clear that God was teaching me His truths the entire time. These stories point to His glory and provision. These stories are intended to encourage you and praise Him.

> *When he came near the place where the road goes down the Mount of Olives, the whole crowd of disciples began joyfully to praise God in loud voices for all the miracles they had seen: "Blessed is the king who comes in the name of the Lord!" "Peace in heaven and glory in the highest!" Some of the Pharisees in the crowd said to Jesus, "Teacher, rebuke your disciples!" "I tell you," he replied, "if they keep quiet, **the stones will cry out.** "*
>
> **Luke 19:37-40 (NIV)**

These stories are the stones of my life crying out! To that end, what He has graciously revealed to me, I now share with you. I pray that these words will encourage you to see yourself in God's story and see where God has always been in yours.

CHAPTER 1:
THE MANURE PILE

It is difficult to believe a story with any spiritual significance could bear this title, I know. Any significance felt can only be perceived in hindsight and, I can assure you, was not completely appreciated when the events occurred. I start with this story because it was the very first story of my childhood that God related to a spiritual truth.

Patty is one of my best friends, and we have known each other since we were six years old. She is one of the most loyal people I have ever known, and as you will soon find out, that loyalty was tested to its limits when we were just ten years old.

Like everyone, I have my strengths. Sense of direction, however, has never been one of them. Long before I was able to drive, I realized that I could not be trusted in this area. Unfortunately, Patty had to learn about my deficiency the hard way.

It was summer. I had just completed fourth grade, and Patty was a year ahead of me. As would often happen, we made our way down to the fields on our dairy ranch. We had crossed the county road from our house, walked down the gravel road passed the hay barn and milking parlor, through several gates and turns, and finally into the field where my dad was perched high on the big cutting machine he called, the Mower. He was easily visible on top of that huge red machine, and when he saw us coming towards him, he stopped his progress so he could talk with us for a while.

The test of the friendship began on our way back to the house. I could see the direction that I needed to go but could not find the path that we took to get to the field. Besides directional weaknesses, I am also not that great at time and distance comparisons, not now nor when I was ten years old. We had not travelled far enough to reach the path back to the house, but my brain began to panic that I must have missed it. Eventually, I decided to improvise.

Improvisation is usually a pretty good skill to have. Unlike navigation, improvisation is one of my strengths! It comes in handy in all kinds of situations. Unfortunately, improvisation can be a liability when one is ten years old and completely lost, on a two-hundred-acre dairy ranch! Improvisation can lead to potentially dangerous circumstances, and in this case, my attempt to improvise a new way home becomes the foundation of my best friend's "Life's Most Embarrassing Moment."

With unfounded and feigned confidence, I led Patty up a path, a much narrower one than the one we should have taken. This path did not go to the house, but instead led to the HUGE manure holding "pond" just below the concrete slab of the corral above. If I could safely navigate us across this barrier, the trip home would be quite short, for on the other side was a slope up to the corral, and from there, I was confident that I could find our way back to the house. The problem was getting across.

Now, before you assume that the manure "pond" was some sort of soup-like consistency, let me remind you that this was in the middle of summer. The hot sun makes manure look crusty and deceivingly stable, almost like concrete, especially to a ten-year-old. The task would be an obvious impossibility without this deception. But in my mind, I thought that it could be done. Surely a couple of little kids could just walk across without disturbing the weathered and greyed surface. So, convinced in my misdirected and unwarranted assurance, I wisely encouraged Patty to go first!

To this day I have no idea why she trusted me. She had only taken a couple of tenuous steps across the pile before she began to sink, and sink, and sink. Right before my tender and guilty little eyes, the scene unfolded a repeat of every childhood imagination and nightmarish replay of every sinking-sand horror movie I had ever seen. I was convinced that I had killed her in the most horrific way. I had been solely responsible for the demise of my best friend in the world: by drowning her in a manure pile!

Patty, the ever calm and rational one of our pairing, instructed me to run back down to the field and get my dad. Oh yeah, the hard-working farmer on the big red machine that I could see from my current vantage point of death and destruction. I ran. I ran hard and fast and blinded by the tears streaming down my cheeks. I could barely see anything in front of me, save the big red blur that was flooded in the haze of my uncontrollable and hysterical tears.

I cannot imagine what my dad was thinking as he saw me flailing after him. What a mess I must have been, but nothing compared to the mess I had created back at the manure pile! I remember crying out to him for help, and I vaguely remember uttering something like, "I've killed Patty! She is sinking in the manure pile!"

I do not remember the look on his face. I'm sure I couldn't have seen his face through all my burning tears, but he immediately came to help. He would fix it all if anyone could and came to the rescue of my doomed friend.

Of course, Dad knew something I did not know. The reality of the situation had, of course, escaped me. The manure pile was only a couple of feet deep and therefore, Patty was not really in much danger of perishing. In fact, when Dad and I reached Patty in her plight, the sinking had ceased, and she was only up to her thighs in the thick, smelly goo. Unfortunately, up to your thighs in manure, although not life-threatening, is still not a situation most people would want to find themselves in. She was safe, but not out!

Getting her out turned out to be quite a trick, however. How does someone pull her out of the thick and stinky muck without themselves getting stuck? My dad had much more weight with which to be concerned. It eventually required a trip up to the barn to obtain a large piece of plywood placed over the gap between where Patty was and where she wanted to be. My dad lay flat on the board to distribute his weight, while he sunk a two-by-four board under her feet. After much pulling on her arms and pushing on the two-by-four, Patty's disgustingly green and smelly self was finally free.

Patty's ordeal and humiliation, however, was not yet finished. We were finally on our way back to the barn on the correct path, Dad leading the way, Patty barely able to bend her legs as the newly exposed manure began to dry. I still remember vividly the red plaid pantsuit she was wearing that day, and the funny monster-walk she was required to use on her way up to the barn as the layer of manure hardened with every step. We finally reached the milking parlor and the humiliation continued. She was now out, but not clean. Dad put her into a metal bucket and took the hose to her and her red plaid outfit.

I am a parent now, and with a parent's perspective, I reflect on that scene and the phone call that invariably had to be made to Patty's parents. It must have been a hoot. It is quite remarkable that her parents let Patty come play at my house ever again, ever. But what could possibly be the spiritual perspective?

No longer ten years old, you would think that my sense of direction would have improved. I can assure you, it has not. On roads and in life, I still get off the track, thinking that I can make my own way and make my own way come out right. The ground on which I walk seems stable enough, but I am easily deceived. Amid it all, I stand to lose my way every time I rely on my own senses and will.

Life happens (or that other famous bumper sticker quote), but in the middle of my misdirected ways, it always helps to have been with God recently. You see, in the sinking of my trusting friend, Patty, I could easily find my way back to Dad riding the big red machine that day. It helped immensely that we had just been with him, talking with him. I couldn't find my way across the manure pile, but I could follow the sound and sight of the machine and my knowledge of where it was, certainly reduced the time required to get help. Our ranch was quite large, and it could easily have been hours before finding someone, (especially since I STILL did not know the right way to go back).

Time with Dad helped me redeem a mess I had made at the manure pile. Time with God does the same.

MEDITATIONS

Trust in the LORD with all your heart,
And lean not on your own understanding;

In all your ways acknowledge Him,
And He shall direct your paths.

Do not be wise in your own eyes;
Fear the LORD and depart from evil.

Proverbs 3:5-7 (NKJ)

Trust God from the bottom of your heart;
don't try to figure out everything on your own.
Listen for God's voice in everything you do,
everywhere you go; he's the one who will keep
you on track. Don't assume that you know it
all. Run to God! Run from evil!

Proverbs 3:5-7 (The Message)

HOMEWORK

Have you ever felt lost in your own life? Confused about how to navigate the latest crisis?

As you have discovered, until the magic and wonder of GPS, or Geographic Positioning System, it seemed like I was always lost. Whether in the middle of a field on our farm, or later when I moved to a city surrounded by lakes and rivers, I've been lost. Before GPS, I would often have to pull over and borrow a phone (before cell phones, too), and call my husband for help. He was born with an internal

GPS, and what was the first question he would ask?

"Where are you now?" What? If I knew the answer to that, I wouldn't be lost! But that is how GPS works... to get where you want to go, you have to know where you are. Check it out. Really. On any GPS application, the system either ASKS you where you are, or it automatically DETECTS where you are. That's it... that's the secret... even when we are talking spiritually. The first step of finding your way anywhere, is to know the place from where you are starting.

So here is the question. Where are you? In relation to Jesus, to His presence (the Spiritual Big Red Mower), where are you? And here is the trick. This only works as an adequate beginning if we are honest in our answer.

1. When was the last time you spent time talking to him?

2. When was the last time you spent time reading His Word?

3. When was the last time you spent worshipping Him?

4. When was the last time you just sat quietly listening for Him?

None of these questions are intended to accuse or make you feel guilty. These are the questions I must ask myself when I am feeling lost, I am feeling alone in my messy life, when I feel like I can't hear His voice, and certainly when I have made a terrible mess and need someone to rescue me. It is not His absence but my proximity to His presence that is an issue. To navigate our way back, we must be honest in where we are now!

If the answer to any of the questions above is "it's been a while," perhaps it is time to get reacquainted with God and His presence. God's presence takes practice. Take another look at the two scriptures. Here's a couple of things you can do to get back on track.

1. Copy one or both scriptures onto a 3x5 card and tape it to your bathroom mirror. Every time you are looking at yourself, take a few minutes to read God's word. Begin and end your days committing His word to memory.

2. Acknowledge Him by writing down THREE things that you are grateful for. Start a list and add THREE new things every day. Keep the list on your mirror and read the growing list every day.

CHAPTER 2:
TANSY WEED

Anyone who does any level of gardening knows that weeds are not good. Since the beginning of time and the incident in the first garden, the battle over the soil has been a persistent one. For my dad, the worst enemy in the fields was the Tansy Weed.

To the untrained eye and to most city-dwellers passing through the valley pastures where I grew up, these yellow blossoms look beautiful from the highway as their vehicles go whizzing by. In some untended fields, it is a stunning carpet of golden sunshine covering the landscape. In their brightest glory, I have seen unknowing travelers parked on the side of the road, taking pictures of this beautiful sight.

My education on tansy started nearly as soon as I could throw on a pair of rubber boots (not those cute, patterned ones they sell to city kids, but the black ones with the red rim at the top) and walk the fields under my own power. I would walk beside my dad, and he would almost unconsciously bend down and pull the immature tansy along whatever path we walked. I learned that it was also my job, possibly my first job, that wherever I walked, I needed to identify the Tansy and pull it, with its roots, out of the ground. The goal was to pull the tansy before its yellow flowers reached their peak and began to seed. Although the weed was easy enough to pull out, it left green and smelly stains on the hand. I didn't like it.

One day, I could not have been more than five or six years old, I asked my dad why it was so important to pull THIS weed. I had noticed that the fields were full of many other types of weeds, and yet my dad never mentioned the need to pull THOSE. Why was the Tansy such a focus of our efforts?

Dad explained that most of the weeds were harmless, but the Tansy was poisonous to the cows. If a cow ate the Tansy, the weed caused the cow to get very sick, and if a cow consumed enough of it, the cow could die. Boy, I suddenly became very aware of all the Tansy along our path!

After a couple of years, I began to wonder why my dad was so casual about pulling the weeds. After all, it seemed to me to make much more sense to hire a big crew of people and comb the entire 200 acres and rid the fields of this nasty and potentially dangerous plant, once and for all! Of course, I shared my brilliant and aggressive idea to my dad. His answer completely surprised me.

"You see, cows won't eat Tansy! They know it is poisonous!" What? Well now my mind was spinning. I started counting how many walks, days, weeks, months, and years I had mindlessly picked the Tansy, and how many years before that, that my dad, mom, and sisters had picked the Tansy. Why? If the cows won't eat it, what is the point? I voiced my incredulity with quite a bit of attitude to my dad, who for some reason, tricked me into picking these stinky, hand-staining weeds for all these years!

There was something more I didn't understand: the nature of Tansy. Tansy is poisonous and it's true that when there is grass to eat, a cow will not touch the poisonous weed. The problem comes when a field is neglected, and no vigilant farmer has plucked out the tansy.

Over a very short amount of time, Tansy will take over a field and choke out everything else that is good for a cow to eat. Left with nothing else, a cow will eat the only food that remains, the Tansy that could kill it.

I posed my final question to Dad. If the cows won't eat the Tansy when there is good grass to eat, doesn't my idea of irradicating the weed in one effort still make more sense? It was then that my dad pointed me in the direction of the river, and more accurately, the fields on the other side of the river. Glowing with the golden blooms of this terrible weed, Dad showed me that not all farmers tended to the Tansy. "See, to be a farmer is to be patient. To be a farmer is to have endurance. The job of pulling Tansy is forever because others do not take care of their fields. Whenever there are fields in the valley with untended weeds, I must be patient and endure. I must be vigilant."

And this is the nature of sin. A single sin does not hold much power, but when left unrecognized and unattended, sin has a way of taking hold and taking over. And the Tansy of Sin is all around my life and yours. Even though I may have managed to keep it at bay in one part of my life, there are fields growing all around me that constantly threaten to take over in other parts. One all-out effort is not the solution to rid my life of sin, but a realization that there will always be tansy in my field, and the goal is to ensure that it does not grow to maturity, fully bloom, and go to seed. Regardless of what others do or do not do, my job is to exercise the farmer's patience, endurance and vigilance and tend my life with God.

Once fertile ground that sustains us, untended sin destroys its surroundings and leaves the human soul with nothing but itself. And our spiritual self gives up its purpose in God and, field by field, acre by acre, relinquishes its ability to feed us. Left with nothing else, our soul feasts on the killer poison that remains.

MEDITATIONS

Here is a trustworthy saying that deserves full acceptance: Christ Jesus came into the world to save sinners—of whom I am the worst. But for that very reason I was shown mercy so that in me, the worst of sinners, Christ Jesus might display his immense patience as an example for those who would believe in him and receive eternal life. Now to the King eternal, immortal, invisible, the only God, be honor and glory for ever and ever. Amen.

1 Timothy 1:15-17

I went past the field of a sluggard, past the vineyard of someone who has no sense; thorns had come up everywhere,the ground was covered with weeds, and the stone wall was in ruins.

I applied my heart to what I observed and learned a lesson from what I saw: A little sleep, a little slumber, a little folding of the hands to rest—and poverty will come on you like a thief and scarcity like an armed man.

Proverbs 24:30-34 (NIV)

CHAPTER 3:
COME BOSS

"C'BAWWWWWW, C'BAWWWWWW!"

It was a sound I grew up hearing every evening. It wasn't an alarm or mill whistle like many of my friends in our little town experienced. What I heard every evening was the sound of my dad's voice calling his cows home for their evening milking. You see, 200 acres is a fairly large space for 100 cows to roam. So, my dad would call out, "C'BAWWWWWW, C'BAWWWWWW!" I wish I could share a recording of how it sounded, but for the longest time I had no idea what my dad was actually saying. I finally asked him, and he translated it to "Come Boss."

Well, it did not sound anything like English to me, but the cows understood it and responded. Wherever they were in the field, no matter how far away they were, the herd turned their heads and hooves toward the barn and started their journey back home, and more specifically, the milking parlor. It was time to be milked. No matter how many other distractions competed for their attention, my dad's voice would cut through the clatter and capture their attention. No matter how thick the delicious grassy food under their feet, they would respond. Even if it was midday and not milking time, if my dad called out to them, the herd turned and followed the sound of his voice.

One day when I was alone in the fields and it was close to milking time, I thought I would give it a try. I could see the herd of cows mingling underneath the oak trees that bordered the riverbank and was confident I could get their attention. With all the breath in my lungs, I bellowed out an impressive "Come Boss," approximating my dad's rhythmic call that I had heard so many times over the years. I anticipated the herd all looking in my direction, a slight pause, and then a lead cow turning in my direction with all the others soon following. And then...

Nothing.

Okay, maybe not exactly nothing. A few ears twitched in my direction, and even a couple heads turned my way. But for the most part, nothing. I gave it another hearty try, and this time, the reaction really WAS nothing. These ladies were not impressed. These dames were not fooled. I was not my dad. I was not their caretaker. They knew his voice; they did not know mine.

With my dad's voice came the predictability of his provision. When his voice sounded, there was safety. When they heard his voice, there would be grain. That voice was there when they were in pain, and with that voice came the assuring touch of his hand. He brushed their sides when he passed, he rubbed and scratched their heads. It was his hand that provided the powder that kept the flies away. Not only did he know them, but they knew him. Not only did those big, brown-eyed ladies belong to him, he belonged to them. They only responded to Dad's voice.

And so, it should be with God and me. He is always calling for me to come, to spend time with him, to leave whatever occupies my attention at the time, turn, and follow Him. At His voice, not only should my ears quicken and my head turn, but also my heart. I should be so familiar to the sound of His voice, that I cannot be fooled by an imposter. I should be so tuned to His calling, that it cannot be drowned out by all the other sounds that fill my life.

And when I turn my attention to Him, there is predictable provision. There is food for my soul to eat and water for my spirit to drink. Every time I turn toward his voice, there is safety. He wants to share both joy and pain with me, and to provide His company and His healing. Time with Him brushes away the distractions and strengthens me for another moment, another day, and another season. In His voice is all things I need. In His voice is provision. In His voice is safety. In His voice is love and acceptance and purpose. My job is to hear His voice, recognize His voice, and respond. In His voice is LIFE!

MEDITATIONS

Come, let us bow down in worship, let us kneel before the Lord our Maker; for he is our God and we are the people of his pasture, the flock under his care.

Today, if only you would hear his voice, "Do not harden your hearts as you did at Meribah, as you did that day at Massah in the wilderness.

Psalm 95:6-8 (NIV)

Very truly I tell you, a time is coming and has now come when the dead will hear the voice of the Son of God and those who hear will live.

John 5:25 (NIV)

CHAPTER 4:
NIGHT RESCUE

There is a certain rhythm on a dairy ranch; cycles of not only seasons, but of days. Dairy cows are milked twice a day to gain the most productivity. If a cow is not milked on that cadence, the cow will slow down in producing milk, which of course, is not beneficial to the profitability of the business. So, morning and night, the cycle continues for farmer and cows.

On a dairy like ours, the number of cows being milked varied during the year, because cows "dry up" right before giving birth, and the goal of the farmer is to ensure all cows are bred and give birth every year. Therefore, a good farmer keeps track of how many cows are expected at each milking. My dad was aware of the count expected to be milked at each milking, to ensure all cows were accounted for.

One evening, however, the count was off. At the end of the milking, we were one cow shy of what my dad expected. A quick look into the holding corral outside the milking parlor confirmed it, there was a cow missing.

Unfortunately, it was already dark and there was still much to do in the barn before anything could be done about the missing cow. Cows do not exactly leave the milking parlor without leaving other things to be cleaned up. While the rest of us scraped and shoveled and sprayed the floors and walls clean, Dad began his search in the fields to find the missing cow. With flashlights in hand, my mom, my sisters and I joined him in the search after our clean-up was complete. It was well into the night and still our efforts had not yielded the missing cow.

Clearly the cow was not in the fields, but with all the fences surrounding the property, where could the cow have gone? Dad decided to troll the river and started up the pull start engine of the little motorboat used for the occasional, and usually not very successful, fishing excursions down the river.

I have a strong and lasting image of my dad, slowly navigating that river with the beam of his flashlight moving back and forth across the surface of the river, beyond the bow of that little boat (so strong, in fact that years after the event, I had a friend of mine draw it for me so I could present it to my dad as a Christmas gift. The image is below). From bank to bank the light moved and eyes were fixed in hopes of detecting anything in the dark river. As Dad trolled the river, the rest of us followed alongside on the bank. Of course, the hope was to find the cow alive, but there was also the dread of a less positive discovery.

I do not remember how long our search lasted, but as a child trudging the muddy riverbank in the dark of night, it seemed like hours. The clay-like mud created a strong suction that threatened to remove my boots with every step. I was cold, wet, and exhausted by the time Dad called out to us that he had found her. The poor lady was knee-deep several yards out into the river with hooves firmly imbedded in the thick and unrelenting clay. The problem for her? The tide was coming in.

More hours of digging, pulling, and trying to keep the cow calm, we were finally successful in releasing the cow from her certain demise of the rising river.

After the trauma subsided, and we were all back home, warm, and dry, I asked Dad why the cow would get herself so far into the river. He paused for a moment, and a thoughtful look of wisdom came across his face. "Cows are stupid!"

Yes, that was it. Cows do not know when it is high or low tide. And cows do stupid things like wander out onto soft clay at low tide, even when there is no grass to eat out there. Cows are heavy, too. It wouldn't take long for the cow's hooves to become buried into the clay, and the clay would be as unforgiving to hooves as they were to my boots. And eventually, low tide becomes high tide, and a cow does not know that either! Cows are stupid!

Years later I began to ponder why Dad even bothered finding the lost cow. He had over 80 other cows that all came home that night, and a new herd of calves coming on every year. What difference would one cow make? But my dad was a "good farmer" who cared about each cow. He knew them, each one of them. He knew their personalities and knew them by sight. He was their caretaker and each one mattered.

Our God is a Good Farmer. He knows each of us by name. He knows when we are in distress and in over our heads. And let's admit it. Left to our own devices, we can get into deep water. Our own intellect and instinct leaves us knee-deep in the mud and muck. Our choices sometimes result in unexpected circumstances. We need a rescue. We need a Rescuer.

And there He is, the God who knows we are lost and He knows when high tide is coming.

MEDITATIONS

Save me, O God,
for the waters have come up to my neck.
I sink in the miry depths,
where there is no foothold.
I have come into the deep waters;
the floods engulf me.
I am worn out calling for help;
my throat is parched.
My eyes fail, looking for my God.

Psalm 69:1-3 (NIV)

In the Same Way your Father in Heaven is not Willing that any should be Lost?

"What do you think? If a man owns a hundred sheep, and one of them wanders away, will he not leave the ninety-nine on the hills and go to look for the one that wandered off? And if he finds it, truly I tell you, he is happier about that one sheep than about the ninety-nine that did not wander off. In the same way your Father in heaven is not willing that any of these little ones should perish.

Matthew 18:12-14 (NIV)

35

CHAPTER 5:
DARK HARVEST

If you haven't already figured out by now, a farmer's kids are pressed into service often and not always during the day light hours. When the town kids were getting ready for baths and bed, there were times when we were putting on our barn clothes and boots. Such was the case one summer night when I was about twelve years old.

Summer on a dairy ranch is an amazing time. It's hay season, and if you like the smell of freshly cut grass, just imagine acres and acres of it. The days are long and full of warm sun, picnics, swims at the lake, and... the rolling of hay bales!

What? Yes, being too small and young to drive the big farm equipment, my job during the summer hay harvest was to roll the bales.

Okay, this could use some additional explanation.

The hay harvest is just a gigantic process by which

farmers store up the cows' food for the coming winter when the fields will be too wet for grazing. There are many steps to this process, and most people only see one or two of the later stages when driving by and seeing the hay bales in the fields, or stacked bales on the hay trucks driving down the road. But long before the final product, several actions occur, and each one requires a unique skill set: The Cut, The Rake, The Baler, The Roll, and the Stack and Haul.

First is the cut. It is nothing like cutting the lawn, by the way. The grass is allowed to grow much longer for hay and is cut once at the base of the stalk, rather than many cuts that would create a sort of mulch. Long stalks allow for the eventual baling process to be successful; you cannot bale small cuts of grass. The cut is accomplished by a huge cutting machine that Dad called the Mower (already mentioned in the first story). If you've ever seen the pattern a Zamboni makes on a hockey rink to refresh the ice surface, that's basically the same pattern used to cut a field (see diagram below).

This pattern is required because the Mower is gigantic and does not have the ability to take tight turns. This pattern allows for the large machine to avoid tight turns and take all turns in the same direction, without leaving any uncut grass. Dad was quite particular about this pattern because he didn't want any of the grass to be missed and lining up the mower row by row is again, much more difficult than mowing your lawn at home.

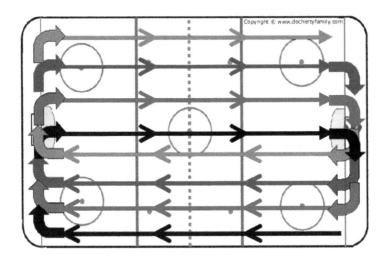

Once the grass is cut, it is left to dry in the field, but the grass can only dry on the side that faces the sun. The grass laying against the ground can get more wet due to the condensation created in the dewy night. Another machine is required to turn over the layers of grass to expose the underside and allow it to also dry in the sun. This machine is the Rake. It takes the same pattern as the Mower, but as the driver, you must continually look backwards to ensure the rake tines are in line with the previously cut row of grass. It's tricky! And again, Dad was not pleased if some of the grass did not get turned.

Once the grass has been fully dried on both sides, The Baler is driven along the patterned rows and its tines scoop up the stocks and pulls them into the machine, which then pushes them with a large "arm" into a bale, wraps it with baling twine, knots and cuts the twine, pushes the completed hay bale out the other end, and then drops it back onto the field. I must admit, I love The Baler, or at least I love watching someone ELSE driving The Baler. It's an amazing piece of machinery, and when in operation, it looks like farming ballet! The rhythm of the arm moving back and forth and the predictable timing of the completed bale thumping to its ground landing is quite artful and satisfying.

In truth, I also hated The Baler because there was a demanding pace required to keep it from jamming. And let's face it. I was an impatient driver. Drive too fast and The Baler would jam with too much hay. Drive too slowly and the bales would end up too light. When I was old enough to run The Baler, I almost always left the baling to someone else... anyone else.

After the field has been completed, the bales are left in the field to continue drying, but again, condensation from the ground leaves the bottom side of the bale too wet, so... they must be rolled! That's right, when you are too young to drive the mower, the rake, or the baler, you get the envious job of rolling bales. That was me.

Not much skill is required, just some protective gloves and a strong set of arms and legs! Row after row, field after field, I would follow the pattern left by the big machines and roll the bales to ensure the underside ended up on top for its last drying. After a day or so in that position, the bales could be loaded and stacked on the truck and hauled up to the barn for storage.

This all sounds so systematic and easy, all on a lovely schedule that works like clockwork, except that in the Northwest, sometimes the weather does not cooperate.

On one summer day, my dad had been watching the weather reports very closely and as he looked out on his fields full of baled and harvest-ready hay, he realized there was going to be a problem. You see, once the hay is baled, it must stay dry until it reaches the barn. If rains come, the bale is ruined and must be broken up and thrown away. Wet bales, besides being too heavy to lift, will mildew and cannot be fed to the cows. So, eyeing the ever-darkening skies, my dad prepared the crew for a long night.

Do not forget, however, that there were also cows that needed to be milked that evening. Certain rhythms cannot be postponed or interrupted. So, dad and a couple of hired hands continued to work the fields as fast as they could, while my mom and sister went back to milk the cows. It was a race to pull in hundreds of bales before the coming storm hit.

Once the cows were milked and the barns cleaned everyone else headed back down to the fields. But by now, it was starting to get dark. There are no streetlights in the fields, so the impending darkness was also going to be a problem. All hands on deck, family and crew worked feverishly to beat the storm. Unfortunately, there is really no such thing as fast hauling of hay! The big hay truck can only go as fast as the two hired hands on the ground can grab, pick up, and throw seventy-five-pound bales up to my dad in the truck. And they can only go as fast as my dad can place the bales securely, so the bales do not fall off on their way up the hill to the hay barn. To have a chance at bringing in all the baled hay that night, we had to have a strategy.

Everyone had a job, a role to play to make it work. My two sisters were rolling hay bales to the two hired hands on the ground to condense the space between bales and keep the strong hired hands throwing instead of searching for the next bale. My mom was driving the hay truck with my dad in the back, and I was driving the little orange pickup behind the truck to provide the light. You see, if the men on the ground cannot see the man in the back of the truck, a flying 75-pound bale could prove disastrous.

Once the truck was full, the bale stack was tied up and the whole crew rode up to the barn, bales were thrown off the truck and restacked neatly and safely protected from the rain. Truck emptied, the whole crew returned to the awaiting fields and the whole process started again.

The darkness came and hour after hour, we brought the hay in. I cannot remember how many truck loads went to the barn that night, but I do remember the last bales were pulled into the barn and my dad let everyone go home without emptying the last truck of its load. We were exhausted, but also exhilarated and relieved that all bales were in before the storm.

I spoke earlier that on a farm, there is a certain rhythm of days and of seasons. Most of the time that rhythm is predictable and planned. But sometimes, there is an interruption to that rhythm. An unexpected event, an approaching catastrophe, a broken fence, a broken machine, or an approaching storm that threatens the crop. In these times, the farmer rallies his resources and meets the challenge with skill, determination, and the sense of urgency required to get the job done. He must because his livelihood and the well-being of his herd and family depend on it. To a farmer and his family, it is the way of life.

The urgency of a storm, the urgency to save the harvest: These are the concerns of not only the farmer in the field, but the farmer who is God. He has a harvest in the field, and there is a storm on the horizon. In most cases, there are many storms on many people's horizons. It is time for everyone who believes to trade their pajamas for work clothes and join the farmer in bringing in the harvest.

Worried that you do not have the right skills? Concerned that you do not possess the right knowledge or education? Maybe you think you are not strong enough or that you are too insignificant to participate in such an important thing. Perhaps there is something in your past or present that keeps you from being part of the crew.

I get it. Remember? I was the little girl whose legs were not long enough to reach the pedals of the big hay truck, whose arms were not strong enough to throw a bale, or whose intellect and experience was not good enough to strategize a plan that summer night. Other people could do those things. The only thing I could do was drive behind in the little orange pickup and shine its headlights in the direction of all the action. That's all. That's it! Compared to the efforts of everyone else, it wasn't much of a job and in the light of day, completely unnecessary. But when darkness came, shining the lights became imperative. It was what I could do and what allowed the other members of the crew to get their jobs done and save the harvest.

If you are a believer, if you really believe that Jesus is the answer to life's storms, then it is time to be part of the crew that brings in the harvest. It is time to stop worrying about what you cannot do, but rather, do what you can do. Get in the pickup and turn on the light. Point the light in the direction of the One who is called the Lord of the Harvest.

If you feel the least bit unqualified due to age, strength, knowledge, experience, or character, remember the first evangelist. No, not John the Baptist or any of the disciples, it was the woman described in John 4, the woman Jesus met at the well.

The woman didn't have much going for her; a checkered past, a checkered present, no Bible degree or pedigree, just a quick meeting and a few words with Jesus and a promise that her waiting for a savior was over. That is all it took for her to run off without her water jar, because the only job she had was to tell others about what and who she had found. And the town immediately made their way to discover what the woman was talking about.

There is an urgency to this harvest. Jesus told his disciples to "look up" when he saw the people from the woman's town coming over the hill to meet him. Their white robes swaying in the breeze must have resembled bright grains of wheat in harvest season. But this was a harvest for Farmer God:

> *I tell you, open your eyes and look at the fields! They are ripe for harvest. Even now the one who reaps draws a wage and harvests a crop for eternal life, so that the sower and the reaper may be glad together. Thus the saying "One sows, and another reaps" is true. I sent you to reap what you have not worked for. Others have done the hard work, and you have reaped the benefits of their labor.*
>
> **John 4:35b-38**

At twelve years old, I was not the one who cut the grass or raked it, I was not the one who baled it, and I was not even among those who loaded it on the truck. But in my own way and within my role, I helped bring in the harvest that night. You can, too. If you believe, you have a story to tell that resembles the woman at the well, that you have met someone who knows everything about you, you can share your story to those waiting to hear. It was enough to convince an entire town to climb the hill and meet Jesus, and that is the same message that will move the hearts of those you know to do the same.

> *How, then, can they call on the one they have not believed in? And how can they believe in the one of whom they have not heard? And how can they hear without someone preaching to them? And how can anyone preach unless they are sent? As it is written: "How beautiful are the feet of those who bring good news!"*
>
> **Romans 10:14-15 (NIV)**

To put in other words, "How, then, can they eat the hay unless someone brought it into the barn? And how can someone bring the hay into the barn if no one drives the truck? And what use is it driving the truck if no one loads it? And how can anyone load the truck if they cannot see the bales or the truck? And how can anyone shine the light for others if they are not called into the field?

You see, there are many jobs and in God's harvest, no job is too small, and no person is without a role to play. All we need to know is what that woman at Jacob's well knew and all we have to express is what she said: "Come, see a man who told me everything I ever did" (John 4:29).

It's dark now, and the rains are coming! So, jump in the driver's seat of that little orange pickup with me and turn on those lights!

MEDITATIONS

In the same way, **let your light shine** *before others, that they may see* **your** *good deeds and glorify* **your** *Father in heaven.*

Matthew 5:16

You, LORD, *are my lamp;* **the** LORD *turns my* **darkness in***to* **light**.

Samuel 22:29

The *people walking* **in darkness** *have seen a great* **light***; on those living* **in the** *land of deep* **darkness** *a* **light** *has dawned.*

Isaiah 9:2

The light shines in the darkness, and the darkness has not overcome it.

John 1:5

When Jesus spoke again to **the** *people, he said, "I am* **the light** *of* **the** *world. Whoever follows me will never walk* **in darkness***, but will have* **the light** *of life."*

John 8:12

I have come **in***to* **the** *world as a* **light***, so that no one who believes* **in** *me should stay* **in darkness***.*

John 12:46

*to open **their** eyes and turn **them** from **darkness** to **light**, and from **the** power of Satan to God, so that **they** may receive forgiveness of sins and a place among those who are sanctified by faith **in** me.*

Acts 26:18

*But you are a chosen people, a royal priesthood, a holy nation, God's special possession, that you may declare **the** praises of him who called you out of **darkness into** his wonderful **light**.*

1 Peter 2:9

CHAPTER 6:
THE TWINS

It's one of my earliest memories. I was probably only three or four years old and there was an event happening in the calf barn. Mom bundled me up in my boots and barn coat and with my sisters, walked me down the driveway, across the road, and over the fence of the calf corral and into the wide-open space inside the barn's lower level. During the warm, summer months, this space was empty, and my sister and I used it for racing our bicycles, but this time of year our antics were not allowed. This was calving season, and all the eminently expectant mothers were kept safe and warm until their time to deliver. In essence, we were peeking into the maternity ward of our dairy ranch.

It was after the evening milking and in retrospect, probably long passed my bedtime. It was an early spring night, and it was already dark outside. Mom led me down the row of calf pens until we reached the wide wooden gate that was closed against the large arena at the end of the

My sisters were tall enough to look over the top of the gate, but I had to kneel and peer through the gap created by the bottom and middle boards. I rested my chin on the rough grey plank and grasped it with both hands, trying to ignore the effect of the cold cement under my knees.

It was such a strange sight inside the arena. Normally filled with several heavily laden cows readying for birth, the arena was empty, save a large mound of hay, my dad, and what appeared to be a miserable mother-to-be laying on the cement floor. Something was wrong.

I'd seen calves being born before. Sometimes the mama stands up, sometimes the mama lays down. Regardless of position, however, there is the obvious effort that one would expect when observing a cow giving birth. Some cows are stoic and silent during the process, others make quite a bit of noise as they push to bring their babies into the world. Even at my young age, I realized that this cow was not acting like a cow ready to give birth.

Don't get me wrong...she was huge! Her belly extended from side to side wider than I had ever seen. She was almost as wide as she was long. Although she was laying down, she was not making any effort, but was listless and weak.

Dad noticed our presence at the gate and asked my mom to come into the arena because he needed help getting the cow up to her feet. I didn't understand what was happening, and I remember Mom turning around and saying something like, "She needs our help, she's having trouble and can't do it alone." Of course, I knew that most cows managed to give birth to their calves without anyone's help. Dad knew the signs of a cow about to "freshen" and would take them out of the regular herd and located them in the safe and warm arena where we were now currently waiting. But sometimes a cow would surprise him and give birth in the night out in the field, clearly without anyone's help.

Mom opened the gate and closed it behind her. Walking past the pile of mounded hay, she grabbed the neck rope that was used to hold the number tag that identified the cow. Then Dad, with all his strength, pushed against the cow and attempted to roll her up onto her hooves. It took several tries of Mom pulling and Dad pushing to finally get her up. Pulling and pushing, they managed to move her forward far enough to get her head into the stanchion (a wooden frame that can be closed to a position that prevents the cow from moving) and closed the board gently against her neck. It would be nearly impossible for the cow to return to her much-preferred laying down position now.

All events so far were puzzling to me, but nothing prepared my little young life for what came next! With the cow firmly held in place by the stanchion, Dad turned to the steaming bucket of water and began washing and scrubbing his hands, wrists, arms and elbows all the way up to his shoulder! This was unusual! I'd seen and participated in the washing needed for milking, but that was only hands and wrists! What in the world was Dad doing?

And then it happened. Without ceremony or warning, my dad put his arm into the cow! He put his arm all the way up to his shoulder into the cow! Honestly, I can still picture it. My instinct was to be horrified and scared, which would normally cause my eyes to squeeze shut to keep from seeing it. But I couldn't. I just stared and wished my mom was still on my side of the fence!

Eventually my dad's arm began to retreat and with it, a tiny pair of shiny black hooves, pointed and perfect. Dad tied each end of a short rope to each hoof and pulled. More time, more effort and then finally, a small brown calf flopped out into Dad's arms. It was limp, which at first seemed normal. Dad peeled the membrane away and carried the calf to the heap of soft hay awaiting. Mama began to cry and struggle against the stanchion, trying to reach her newborn baby, but her job was not done.

Believe it or not, another washing from fingertip to shoulder, and my dad returned to the cow for another round. Same process, but this time it was taking longer, and all the while I was keeping my eye on the calf on the hay, awaiting the sign of life, the opening of the eye and a sway of the head, but nothing. Dad's second excursion released another calf and another trip to the mound of hay. More crying from the mama, but now she could finally be released from the head hold.

Two beautiful and perfect calves, and the mama cow, freed from her predicament, gently and persistently licking her new babies. It was all back to normal now, except the mama became more and more persistent. Licking and pushing, nudging, and poking, but with no movement from either baby. Her babies were dead. I remember being so sad for the mama. All that work, and I'm sure expectation, and nothing to show for it.

Dad let the cow linger but eventually led her out of the arena and into the open air with the rest of the herd. My mom cleaned up and put her coat back on, and slowly led us away from the warmth of the barn and into the night.

There is probably no stronger memory of my childhood then the sight of that mama trying to bring life to her babies. The expectation and promise and the realization that there was no reward for the long effort.

Maybe it's a little weird, but every time I feel disappointment, where my dreams or expectations have not been realized, I see the image of that mama and the empty pile of hay after the babies were removed. In fact, the pile of hay is the image of unrealized dreams for me.

Maybe you do not have such a striking image, but I cannot believe I am alone in that feeling when something goes completely sideways, completely against expectations, there is the feeling of such immense loss that it shakes our faith in God and our future.

Now that I am all grown up, I can assure you that the delayed or broken promises, betrayals, and unmet expectations in my life have brought me back to that image at the hay pile many times. My instinct is to hover over the disappointment and sometimes I can even feel stuck, not able to move on from that sad and painful place.

This is grief. The mourning over what could have been keeps us from taking steps forward. We stand weakened and paralyzed, afraid to let go. But the Good Farmer is there, graciously waiting for our tears and frustration to subside. If we can trust, just one more time, He will lead us into the open air of His presence and a return of hope, strength, and trust.

MEDITATIONS

For I know the **plans** *I have for you,"*
declares the Lord, *"***plans** *to prosper you and*
not to harm you, **plans** *to give you hope and*
a future.

Jeremiah 29:11

Why, my soul, are you downcast? Why so
disturbed within me? Put your **hope** *in God,*
for I will yet praise him, my Savior and my
God.

Psalm 42:5, 42:11, 43:5

but those who **hope** *in the* Lord *will renew*
their strength. They will soar on wings like
eagles; they will run and not grow weary,
they will walk and not be faint.

Isaiah 40:31

But as for me, I watch in **hope** *for the* Lord,
I wait for God my Savior; my God will hear
me.

Micah 7:7

CHAPTER 7:
WRONG PLACE, WRONG TIME

Cows are jumpy. Cows are persnickety. Cows do not like the unexpected. When things do not go exactly as expected, cows stop giving milk. In and around the milking parlor, everything is done to keep those ladies calm so they will "let down" their milk.

When I was still too young to help milk the cows, I would often want to join my mom and dad in the milking parlor and watch the cows being milked, but I had to sit at the end of the parlor and not make any noise or fidget, as a little kid is prone to do. I was not familiar to the cows; I did not belong. My presence, and particularly my unexpected movement, might cause problems.

As I got older and tall enough to work the grain lever (a spring-loaded device that lets down a measured amount of grain for each cow), I began to join in the milking process (although not nearly often enough according to my sisters). There is a rhythm in the milking parlor, just like everywhere else on the dairy. I can still hear the percussion sounding beats of the air intake, back and forth, as the suction was created through the pipes and down to the milking machine hanging on the hook at each stanchion. Woosh Woooosh, Woosh Woooosh. The rhythm resembled that of a heartbeat.

Morning after morning, evening after evening, the milking machines were started, buckets were filled with iodine-filled hot water, and the rope connected to a pulley system that opened the barn door was pulled down to let in the first three cows. Of course, the first cows, anxious to get the grain that awaited them, shoved, and pushed their way in. The trick was letting go of the rope at just the right time so that the sliding barn door would shut right behind the third cow and before the fourth cow was in the parlor. When the cows are rushing the door, this was tricky!

Each cow would head into an open stanchion, the rear gate was swung closed, allowing the second cow to move passed and into the second stanchion. Once the second cow was in and her rear gate closed, the third cow could reach her slot.

The cows' udders were immediately washed, and machines were removed from their hooks and placed on the cows. These machines were efficient, and within ten minutes, the job was complete. Then, the machines were removed and hung back on the hooks. The front gates of each stanchion were opened and the cows exited the parlor, making room for the next group. Of course, there is much pooping that occurs in the parlor during this process, and if the cows are nervous for any reason, they poop more… sometimes a lot more!

One evening milking, things went terribly wrong in the pooping department. Every cow came in jittery and showed their displeasure not just by pooping, but by projectile pooping. Every cow. Are we talking about poop again? Yes, we are!

As the evening progressed, it got worse and worse. Every time we pulled down the rope to slide open the door, cows rushed in, slipping out of control on the pavement, trying to escape the corral.

About half-way through, my dad had had enough and decided to investigate the situation. He climbed up the narrow concrete stairs leading out of the pit, wrapped his hands around the edge of the rough wood door, and slid it open. I held the door open with the rope, and Dad trudged out amongst the angry mob of ladies, slipping all over, seemingly trying to find their way out of that corral.

And there it was… an unusual face among those big, brown-eyed jersey cows, peeking over the back of one of her corral mates. A deer had somehow made her way into the crowded corral and upset everything.

This deer did not belong, and it was unclear how this

lovely, delicate, and graceful creature managed to get in with this unruly, gangly, and clumsy group of women waiting to be relieved of their milk load. Now that the source of all the commotion and disruption was known, my dad had another problem. How do you remove a wild deer out of the corral without losing all the remaining cows? As with most wild animals, it seems much easier for them to get INTO a situation than it is for them to get OUT.

Dad asked me to close the sliding barn door, so I have no idea what he tried out there, but after about ten minutes, the door slid back open, my dad slipped through and let the door slide back to its closed position. I do remember, however, that he was a mess and looked exhausted and defeated. The result of his efforts? Nothing. The deer was still in the corral, and the cows were still quite upset with the disruption. Basically, we continued to milk the cows, with Dad having to return to the corral many times, to herd the cows into the barn three at a time. It was a long, and messy night.

More poop and more spiritual lessons, I know. There is the obvious one already mentioned, of course. It is always easier to get into a mess than it is to get out of one. But I'm saving that lesson for a later story!

This story's lesson comes from my dad's response and his efforts to solve the problem. Although he tried to eradicate the problem by removing the offending deer, he was not successful, but he didn't really give up, either. After many attempts, he came back to the parlor and resumed the milking! I'm not sure I would have done that. I would have been tempted to just open the corral gate and let out the cows and their unwanted guest, go home and get clean, and start over the next morning. Yep, I'm pretty sure that would have been the only strategy I could have come up with.

Here's the difference. I was just the farmer's kid. I was focused on getting home and getting cleaned up. I was hungry and tired, and all my focus was on those things. I was the farmer's kid and not the farmer.

The farmer, amid a seemingly impossible situation, doesn't lose sight of the bigger picture or the bigger job. His job that night was to get all the cows milked. That was his job every morning and night, and the job didn't change just because there was a deer in the corral.

Oh, how many times I lose track of the bigger picture and the bigger job, especially when things are not going as planned. I can become sidelined by circumstances, distracted by derailments, and focused on my frustration and failure to cope and complete. In fact, I use that phrase too much in my day to day internal conversation... "I'm so frustrated!"

I wish I could have been in my dad's mind that night, following his thought processes through to his conclusion, but I can at least imagine it. After all, he did attempt to remove the distraction, but after only ten minutes, he was back in the milking parlor and returning to his primary purpose. It took longer, it was messier, but we finished the job.

Ever feel like there is a deer in your corral, stirring up trouble and causing a mess to your neat and ordered life? The errant deer can come in all kinds of forms: a lost job, a lost relationship, a missed deadline, a missed recognition. It is that helpless feeling when things are out of my control that causes the most distress and distraction, that causes me to look in a different direction, forget, and lose focus. I take my eyes off my purpose and forget what my purpose is. The good news is that we are not alone.

- Abraham and Sarah got distracted by how long it was taking for God to answer their prayers and His promises.

- Jacob got sidelined by his ambition.

- Joseph's brothers were overwhelmed by competition and jealousy.

- Moses got frustrated by the nagging and complaining of an ungrateful people who blamed him for everything going wrong.

- David got distracted by someone else's pretty wife and his need to cover up his own deeds.

The Bible is full of people distracted by unexpected circumstances. From the beginning to the end of God's story, people are always dealing badly with an unexpected deer in their corral. Their purpose and calling get lost in the mayhem of their current situations. Amid their troubles, they lose sight of their God.

God's people haven't changed much. Somehow, with amazing patience and grace, God breaks through the distraction and gets us back on track. Thankfully, God gets us. He gets our tendency to be overwhelmed. His presence and His word draws us back and gives us the courage to press on until the job is done.

MEDITATIONS

His divine power has given us everything we need for a godly life through our knowledge of **him** *who* **called** *us by his own glory and goodness.*

2 Peter 1:3

See what great love the Father has lavished **on** *us, that we should be* **called** *children of God! And that is what we are! The reason the world does not know us is that it did not know* **him**.

1 John 3:1

Create in me a pure heart, O God, and renew a steadfast spirit within me. Do not cast me from your presence or take your Holy Spirit from me. Restore to me the joy of your salvation and grant me a willing spirit, to sustain me.

Psalm 51:10-12

CHAPTER 8:
CHICKEN WIRE
(GROSS OUT WARNING)

Have you ever heard of Charles Barnard? I hadn't heard of him either, but he is the brilliant and resourceful guy who invented chicken wire in 1844. He just happened to be an ironmonger living in a cloth weaving town and utilized weaving techniques to create a very effective material to protect small animals from predators. Well done, Charles!

We didn't raise chickens on our dairy ranch. We had the

occasional pet rabbits, a couple of dogs over the years, lots of barn cats and only one house cat, but never chickens. My education of chickens occurred many years later when living in the suburbs! Within our city limits, we were allowed to keep half a dozen chickens, but only if there were no roosters!

Here is what you need to know about chickens. Chickens are fun to raise, they are pretty social and will follow you around like little old ladies, they make great weed eaters but will devour any berry plants you might also be trying to grow, they give you fresh eggs daily, and they are always on their way to finding a way to die. Yes, that's right. Everything living out in the world is looking for a fresh chicken to eat, and as their owner, it's a constant battle of wits and wills to keep chicken enemies at bay. Needless to say, it was a full-time job fortifying their coop to keep them safe. Needless to say, we have lost many a chicken in the multiple attempts.

Living in a suburban neighborhood, the enemies are generally racoons, and it is no accident that they look like bandits. Cute as they are, they can be vicious and oh, so very clever in devising ways to penetrate the chicken fortress. Our property, although fenced, backed up against a forest full of predators. Raids and racoon armies circled the coop nightly, I'm sure, looking for a gap, a breach, a weakness. As their caretakers, we had to find ALL the gaps, and as the predators, they only had to find ONE!

Chapter 8: Chicken Wire (Gross Out Warning)

Recently we left our suburban neighborhood and moved to a much more rural area and yes, we still wanted chickens. But now, we are surrounded by acres and acres of forest, and in that forest are not only racoons, but coyotes. My neighbor lost her entire chicken flock to coyotes who dug around three feet of wire under her coop. Season by season, it seemed the predators were getting bolder and bolder in their efforts to get their desired chicken dinner. I once even interrupted a coyote in the middle of the day, crossing our circular driveway, on his way to visit the chickens and see what damage he could do.

Well, we lost a lot of chickens, and with each attack, we attempted to strengthen the boundaries between our little flock and the outside. We started with a dog kennel, one of those ten-foot square heavy wire structures. We thought we had really figured out a good solution. We were wrong.

One morning I went out to check on them and was devastated to see that five of my eight chickens had been massacred. I do not know if it was racoons or coyotes, but the chickens were still in the coop, every one of them without their heads. The predators had pulled their heads out between the holes of the dog kennel wire. Kennel wire is not chicken wire. Charles Barnard would be ashamed of us!

We quickly realized what had happened. The kennel wire, small enough to keep the chickens inside, was not small enough to keep the chickens' heads inside! Gross, I know, but we immediately understood why chicken wire is made the way chicken wire is made!

Charles had figured it out! The 1-inch hole created by the clever weaving process is too small for the adult chicken to poke her entire head through. She might be able to push part of her beak through, but she is unable to go farther.

Charles clearly knew more about chickens than we did. He knew that chickens have terrible instincts when danger is lurking about. Remember, the coop is ten-feet-squared! When a coyote or racoon comes to visit on the boundary of their coop, all the chickens could easily evade their hungry enemies by huddling together in the middle of the coop. They would be completely out of reach and safe from danger.

Ahhh, but that is not what chickens do! In fact, the chicken's instinct is to immediately run to the edge of the coop and stick their necks out! In the face of danger, they run toward it in attempts to get away from it. It's crazy! And of course, as soon as they have their heads out of protection, the predator grabs them and attempts to pull them out. Not successful, they leave with merely a snack of a chicken head, leaving the whole chicken dinner on the other side. Regardless, the damage is done.

When trouble comes, my instincts are usually not any more reliable. When danger is lurking on the edges of my life, my instincts tell me to run for freedom, to panic, to fret, to escape. When I am feeling alone, I run for more loneliness, isolation, and independence. When feeling vulnerable, I escape to self-protection. When temptation circles my soul, I seek the protection of secrecy and darkness. I can do this myself; I can do this alone. I convince myself I am clever enough and strong enough to survive life's predators. Just like the chickens', my instincts are wrong. Every natural inclination I have in times of distress take me away from the center, away from the flock, away from safety.

Yes, we get it wrong. Some people think God and his expectations of our behavior is a cage to keep us locked up, to prevent us from living, to remove fun and excitement from our lives. In reality, it is His fortress to keep the enemy of our soul out. Within His love and will, there is safety. Within His boundaries, there is opportunity to live another day. The next time trouble comes your way, remember the chicken wire and run to the middle, stay with the others, and be safe in God's protection.

MEDITATIONS

*My tears have been my food
day and night,
while people say to me all day long,
"Where is your God?"
These things I remember
as I pour out my soul:
how I used to go to the house of God
under the protection of the Mighty One[a]
with shouts of joy and praise
among the festive throng.*

*Why, my soul, are you downcast?
Why so disturbed within me?
Put your hope in God,
for I will yet praise him,
my Savior and my God.*

Psalm 42:3-5

*Whoever dwells in the shelter of the Most
High will rest in the shadow of the Almighty.
I will say of the Lord, "He is my refuge and
my fortress, my God, in whom I trust."*

*Surely he will save you from the fowler's
snare and from the deadly pestilence.*

Psalm 91:1-3

CHAPTER 9:
PIT FALL

This chapter is going to require a little background and graphics before we get to the story. I am aware that most of my readers will not be familiar with the operations or even the definition of a "milking parlor," and even fewer will know that many parlors have a pit in the middle. I'm going to attempt to illuminate what our milking parlor looked like because it is important to the story.

Above is a picture of a milking parlor (much larger than ours), but you can see that on each side are the stanchions where the cows stand, and down the middle is a lowered area where a person or persons stand. At each stanchion, there is a milking machine connected to two hoses: one that supplies the suction and the other that collects the milk. All of this is connected to a pipe system that runs all the collected milk into a holding tank. The machine itself is a clever bit of technology, too. When the "cups" are hung on hooks at each station, the cups face down and air flow is cut off. As soon as you tip the cups up, suction begins again and the machine is placed on the cow, and voila, automated milking begins!

Our parlor was much smaller and only had room for six cows at a time, three on each side, with a sunken pit in the middle. Cows are let into the parlor three at a time and the farmer moves from side to side. When the three cows on one side are connected and milking, he finishes up on the other side, removes their machines, and swings open a gate to let them out and the stanchion is prepared for the next three.

The pit allows the person milking to be at eye level with the cow's bag instead of having to bend down and place the machine. This ingenious design has saved many a farmer's back over the years! But of course, that's not this story!

Cows get very enthusiastic when the sliding barn door opens. The earlier cows are particularly aggressive, because they know there is grain awaiting them in the milking parlor. When the door opens, they push and shove to be one of the next three to be let in. It's a cow's version of a Black Friday department store sale on the day after Thanksgiving.

And now for the story.

One night (disasters always seemed to strike during the evening milking), my mom and I were milking because my dad was out of town attending a bowling tournament. As expected, the first cows were pushing and shoving themselves aggressively through the door at each opening and it was tricky to get the door shut before unwanted cows made their way in. We were doing well, though. For a while.

Then, I pulled on the rope that slid the big door open. One of the younger cows came in so quickly and out of bodily control, that her hooves began to slip on the concrete. Unfortunately, there just isn't anywhere to go, and once traction is lost, well, there's nowhere to go! So, in she came, all hooves and panic, as she slid into the first stanchion nearest the door. She slid in, fell to her knees, and kept on sliding. She ran out of concrete as she reached the ledge and fell headlong into the pit below. Of course, NOW she could get traction and immediately stood up, confused, and extremely agitated.

Try to picture it. The only way out of the pit is the very narrow stairs built for humans. There is so much wrong with this scenario, but suffice it to say, cows are not accustomed to climbing stairs, but even if she was willing, she would not fit through the human-sized opening at the top of the steps. She was stuck in a place she was never supposed to be, and my mom and I were now stuck with an entire herd of cows waiting to be milked. Remember that cows are not happy when things are out of place. A cow in the pit is definitely out of place.

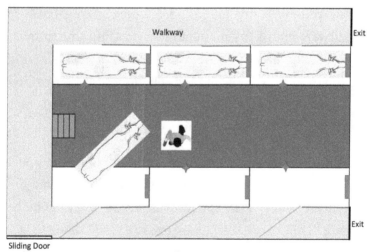

Even if we could get her through the opening, there is no way the two of us were strong enough to coax her up those stairs, and she was much too heavy to push her back up from where she came.

Mom and I were hovering between laughing hysterically and crying uncontrollably. At some point, knowing Dad was not available for a rescue, my mom sent me back to the house to call my grandpa for help. He lived about 20 minutes away and could come and assess the situation. We needed a miracle.

Grandpa showed up, and all I remember is the funny look on his face as he shook his head in disbelief. In the meantime, Mom had attempted to milk the remaining cows by herself. Short-term solution? Milk the rest of the cows and get them back in the pasture. So, we did. Working around the misplaced cow, occasionally moving her substantial girth, we milked the remaining and very upset cows, all the while trying to keep them calm even though there was an obvious and disruptive sight of one of their sister cows in the pit.

Eventually we cleared all the cows from the parlor and tried to strategize how to get the cow out of her unfortunate situation. We attempted to push her back up into the stanchion from whence she came, but she was not having it. No amount of our strength and her girth and anxiety was going to make a difference.

Finally, after many failed attempts, the bars around the stair opening were eventually removed completely, and with much force, the errant cow was maneuvered up the narrow steps and back to the upper level. Yes, for the first time in my life, I was witnessing a cow climb steps. After all of that, she still needed to be milked! She was milked and set free. What a night!

Immediately after my dad returned and heard the harrowing story, new bars were installed at cow ankle level to prohibit any future catastrophes. Any future cow who might slip and fall on the cement floor, would slide into that lower bar and be stopped from falling into the pit below. A hurt ankle on her side was easier to right than a cow on her feet in the pit.

This life is fraught with mishaps. In my exuberance to obtain something I desire, I can slide headlong into disaster and find myself in a pit from which I cannot climb out. In most decisions that have landed me in a place in which I did not belong, I could not escape by just simply reversing my course. And have you ever noticed how much easier it is to get IN to trouble than it is to get OUT of it? Sometimes the pit in which I find myself is too deep and too steep to get out on my own. It takes a miracle. It takes an Intelligence beyond my own to escape.

God, just like my grandpa that night, has tools and strategies that I do not possess. When I rely on Him, he patiently finds a way to move the substantial girth of my lack of knowledge and experience and lifts me out of my circumstances. He miraculously removes the narrow and restrictive barriers that keep me from safety. He manages to move me through steps that my feet are not accustomed to climb. It is hard to trust. It is hard to climb. But when I am back where I belong, He also takes measures to protect me from my next fall, because our God is a good God. Our God is a good farmer.

Meditations

I have told you these things, so that in me you may have peace. In this world you will have **trouble**. *But take heart! I have overcome the world.*

John 16:33

The LORD *is a refuge for the oppressed, a stronghold in times of* **trouble**.

Psalm 9:9

You are my hiding place; you will protect me from **trouble** *and surround me with songs of deliverance.*

Psalm 32:7

But I will sing of your strength, in the morning I will sing of your love; for you are my fortress, my refuge in times of **trouble**.

Psalm 59:16

He will call on me, and I will answer him; I will be with him in **trouble**, *I will deliver him and honor him.*

Psalm 91:15

Therefore do not worry about tomorrow, for tomorrow will worry about itself. Each day has enough **trouble** *of its own.*

Matthew 6:34

Peace I leave with you; my peace I give you. I do not give to you as the world gives. Do not let your hearts be **troubled** *and do not be afraid.*

John 14:27

I have told you these things, so that in me you may have peace. In this world you will have **trouble**. *But take heart! I have overcome the world.*

John 16:33

CHAPTER 10:
TARGET 1 – THE BIT

Over the years of growing up on the dairy, there was a small parade of different types of animals on the ranch besides the cows and bulls. There were a couple of dogs, many barn cats, one house cat named Sidney, a couple of rabbits, and several horses. The horse of greatest prominence was Target. She was mostly dark brown in color, except her legs and face were bright white. And in the middle of her white forehead, she had a unique marking; a nearly perfect brown circle surrounded by a larger grey circle, making it look like… you guessed it, a target.

Now before you think that every horse on a diary ranch would be a work horse, think again. Target was rarely pressed into duty. No, she was a pet. She had a certain elevation of status on our property, and the older she got, the more status she obtained for herself.

Oh yes, when we first bought Target, we rode her quite a lot. My mom loved riding horses, and of course, learning to saddle and ride a horse was a required skill. I'm not exactly sure why we had a horse, other than pleasure, since Target was never used for anything purposeful on the ranch. Riding a horse was just for the pleasure and recreation of it. Pleasure and recreation for the rider, not pleasure for Target.

You see, Target preferred to spend her time leisurely walking around on the hillside just above our house, eating grass, taking long naps in the afternoon, and arising only to the sound of the approaching grain bucket that one of us provided for her every night. Seriously, it was ridiculous, and she was spoiled.

After all, Target was a horse, and sometimes someone on the ranch would want to go for a ride. You would think there would be a measure of gratitude for the nightly bucket of grain and the beautiful living arrangement that we provided for her. You would think, out of such gratitude, that she would willingly grant any of her benevolent caretakers a nice ride on occasion. Not so.

If you wanted to ride Target, you could not be so foolish as to just boldly approach her with a rope and expect her to stand still and be caught. One had to be covert and approach her open-handed or better yet, having bucket of grain in hand. When Target saw the bucket and heard the grain rattling inside, she had a problem. She was really smart. She knew that if the bucket was being presented at any other time than evening, it was only there as a lure.

If she succumbed to the lure, she would be caught. Once caught, the bucket would be taken away, replaced with a bit and saddle.

The problem for Target? She could resist anything but grain. Of all the grain buckets that came her way in her lifetime, she had to have known the possibility of the trap. And of all those buckets, she resisted none of them. As you approached with grain held out in front and a rope hidden behind your back, you could almost see the gears in her brain turning, calculating, strategizing ways that she could get her substantial nose into that grain bucket and consume all the grain inside, and get out and away before the rope could catch her around the neck. But, alas, once her nose was in the bucket, she did not have the will to remove it. The pull of the grain was always too much for her and invariably the indulgence would result in her capture. After the capture, the saddle and bit were soon to follow, which always resulted in having to carry a load she did not want to carry for distances she did not want to travel.

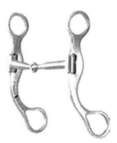

Now don't misunderstand. There is nothing painful about the bit and little discomfort in the saddle for a horse.

It is a matter of control. You see, a horse is tremendously strong and completely capable of overcoming any attempt at force by a rider. The fact of the matter is, between a horse and a rider, it is an unfair match. The strength and speed of a horse will always overcome a person. Except when there is a bit. It is a metal bar that rests inside the horse's mouth and when the attached reins are moved to the left, the pressure of the bit turns the horse's head and with that small change, the direction of the entire horse moves to the left. Move the reins to the right, the entire horse will move to the right.

The point? Five inches of metal can control 1,000 pounds of horse! And the spiritual lesson of this story is this. I am not Target; I am not a horse. I need to be smarter than Target. I need to know what happens when I succumb to what appears to be a trap attached to whatever it is I have difficulty resisting. Because just like Target, once my nose is firmly supplanted in the "grain" of whatever I desire, I can immediately feel the tether encircling my neck. The ability to retreat to safety wanes and no amount of willpower can get me out of the predicament.

You see, we all wear spiritual "bits." Some are good for us; they can change our direction in unexpected and positive ways. They can move us in the direction of productivity and contribution and promise. Other desires are not good for us. They can act on our souls like the bit in a horse's mouth. A small thing that moves us into paths of captivity, taking us in directions we didn't intend to go.

And that is the way of sin. It's just a small thing really. A little desire, a little distraction. And the little thing, given enough control over our lives, takes us away from God's path, away from our purpose in Him. I repeat: we all wear a Spiritual bit! The question to ask ourselves is… Who is holding the reins?

MEDITATIONS

Endure hardship as discipline; God is treating you as his children. For what children are not disciplined by their father? If you are not disciplined—and everyone undergoes discipline—then you are not legitimate, not true sons and daughters at all. Moreover, we have all had human fathers who disciplined us and we respected them for it. How much more should we submit to the Father of spirits and live! They disciplined us for a little while as they thought best; but God disciplines us for our good, in order that we may share in his holiness. No discipline seems pleasant at the time, but painful. Later on, however, it produces a harvest of righteousness and peace for those who have been trained by it.

Hebrews 12:7-13

"There are many types of bits for many different disciplines, but the severity of ALL bits lies in the hands holding them."

—Monty Roberts (horse trainer)

CHAPTER 11:
TARGET 2 – THE SADDLE

Now that you've had a little introduction to our horse, Target, it must be emphasized that she was a very nice horse. It also must be emphasized that, as nice as she was, she also had her opinions and preferences. As stated before, her daily preference was to wander her hillside pasture unencumbered by riders. But once caught, she was a gentle horse who acquiesced to the demands placed on her for short periods of time, but not without a trick or two.

I told you she was smart. She was also sneaky and clever. Remember my best friend who ventured ahead in the manure pile? Well, she plays into this story as well. You see, Patty didn't have a horse to ride at her house. This means that whenever she was at my house and we were trying to decide what to do, the invariable answer was, "Let's ride Target!"

When we were younger, riding the horse required the assistance of either a parent or one of my older sisters, so of course, the request to ride Target was not always granted. But once in a while, Patty would get her wish and the process of catching and preparing Target for a ride would begin.

You already know the process for capture, and yes, this process would be required every time. But once caught and bit was in Target's mouth, the rest was fairly easy and without incident... sort of.

Target would be tied to a fence or gate by the reins, and one of the adults or near adults would drape the saddle blanket across Target's back and begin the process of applying the saddle. Not a problem. Target would wait patiently as the saddle was placed on top of the blanket and the girth strap cinched up tight against her fore belly. The rule was that the cinch needed to be tight, but not so tight that you could not run your flat hand between the girth and Target's belly. So of course, my older sister ensured that the saddle was snug but not pinching. Mission accomplished.

Oh yeah... here comes the sneaky, smart part. Patty and I were hoisted up by using the stirrups and a little shove from the sister. One rider in front seated in the seat part of the saddle, the other rider behind. We were young and light, and generally the two of us probably weighed the same amount as one adult rider. Not a problem.

The intent was that once seated on top of Target, my sister would take the reins and lead us around the upper hillside pasture. A nice easy walk around, then back to the house. Unfortunately, Target had other plans. I believe we got to about three steps forward, and immediately Patty and I knew there was something wrong. Yep... first slowly and then quite quickly, the saddle began to shift sideways. Before we could yell out to my sister to stop, the saddle had slid all the way to the side and dumped us onto the ground. And there the saddle hung, nearly inverted with the seat hanging below Target's belly.

Target had held her breath and expanded her belly to its capacity during the cinching process and only after we were seated and on our way, did she release her breath, causing her belly to decrease in size and making the cinch no longer effective in keeping the saddle upright. With the load of the two girls, it took no time for gravity to take hold and turn us off.

Unfortunately for Target, that trick can only work once. From that point on, we would saddle and cinch her, then walk her around the yard a bit, and then tighten up the cinch again to ensure the saddle was tight. Lesson learned!

No matter how hard Target tried, she couldn't hold her breath forever. Eventually, the effort of walking around required her to let her breath out and her belly in. And once we had her saddled correctly, we had the assurance that we could ride her without mishap of the saddle.

I don't know if you ever feel like you're holding your

breath, waiting for something to happen that resembles effectiveness, but I do. I am hesitant at the burden that awaits me, not sure of myself or events on the horizon. So, I wait; I hold my breath. If only I would just relax. To be called a Servant of Christ is to be called a SERVANT. To serve is to carry a burden: a burden ordained by God for me to carry. And I wait, I am not sure, and I find ways to avoid the burden. I say that the burden does not fit, I cannot hold it. I hold my breath and puff out my spiritual belly and only pretend that I am willing to hold the load I have been given. I won't even let myself take a few steps, because unlike Target, I can hold my spiritual breath for a long time.

MEDITATIONS

Come to me, all who are heavy burden, I will give you rest. My yoke is easy.

Matthew 11:28 (The Message)

CHAPTER 12:
TARGET 3 – THE TREE

One more story about this amazing horse. When she was successfully saddled and the cinch was securely tightened around her girth, Target was a very pleasant horse to ride. But one summer afternoon, my sister Debbie decided that we would ride her together without the benefit or hassle of the saddle. We were going to ride bareback.

Let me tell you that there is some added security in riding a horse with a saddle. The seat provides stability and there are stirrups that provide leverage for your feet and legs. If the stirrups are at the correct length for the rider, it allows the rider to slightly lift out of the saddle for even more leverage when needed, usually when the horse is trotting or even at a dead run. When riding double, the back rider also has something stationary to hold on to, other than the rider in front. The lip of the saddle seat makes for a great handle!

But again, Debbie wanted to ride Target together

without the saddle. No problem. Okay, I must admit it: The thought of riding up and down the hillside without the security of a saddle worried me. I was much younger and a less experienced and far less confident rider than my sister. And besides, Mom didn't like us to ride without a saddle on the hillsides. But Debbie was enthusiastic, and Mom wasn't looking. And truthfully, I trusted her. She was the older sister. No problem.

And in the beginning of our ride, there WAS no problem. We started up the hill, my arms wrapped tightly around Debbie's waist with her urging Target to keep a nice walking pace. And from our vantage point on top of Target, the view of the fields and river down below were stunning. You can almost hear the movie music playing in the background, as we gracefully moved along our path, with grass beneath us and blue sky above us, and the sunshine warming our backs.

Okay, enough of the poetry, now time for reality. Yes, it was lovely and idyllic, but as we progressed up the hill, Target began to pick up her pace and I began to get nervous. I asked Debbie to slow down, and she assured me that she was trying to slow down. She began to pull back hard on the reins to slow Target's pace, but uncharacteristically, Target did not yield. In fact, the more my sister pulled back on the reins, the more earnest Target was in her acceleration.

At first, it was not evident to me what was going on. I was smaller than my sister, and since I was riding behind her, could not see what was ahead of us. But I could hear Debbie, now with some urgency in her voice, talking to Target, or rather, yelling at Target. No longer just trying to slow the horse down, Debbie was now in full effort to get the horse stopped. I started to panic.

And then I saw it. As I poked my head around my sister's shoulder while straining to keep my body on the horse and keep my grip on my sister, I saw it. The giant oak tree that was perched on the hillside and overlooked the valley view below. Normally, a beautiful and majestic sight, now the tree loomed ominous. And not so much the entire tree, but specifically the large lowest branch that hung out to the right side of the tree. The branch was just high enough for Target to walk under and just low enough to disallow anything riding on top of Target to pass. And Target was now heading right for it and at quite a clip.

Regardless of my sister's efforts, Target reached the tree limb, trotted under it, and Debbie and I were swiftly wiped back and over Target's ample rump and deposited firmly onto the ground. We were headed up hill, so the ground was even farther away than normal. After rolling off and recovering, we both looked up to see the quite satisfied Target, casually looking our way from the other side of the limb as she lowered her head to munch on a bit of grass. We had been successfully "treed."

The ride was over. Debbie rushed to see if I was going to live and then helped brush off the dirt from my clothes.

We sheepishly returned to the house hoping we would not get into too much trouble with Mom.

You know that saying: Whenever you fall, get back up again! Although I indeed got back up from the ground, it took some time before I was willing to get back up to ride Target again. Long after the bumps and bruises from our crash landing were healed, I kept my distance and sidelined an activity that up to that point, I had absolutely loved. I was afraid. If my sister couldn't keep me safe on a horse, how was I going to manage it?

Eventually, I returned to horse riding, but from that time forward, any riding excursions, with or without a saddle, took a wide berth away from that tree.

And the spiritual lesson? We all fall. Whether in our physical activities, our personal or professional lives, in missing goals or forgetting to ever make them... we fall.

When we are young, our earliest lessons are encouraged by others to get back up. From the time we attempt our first unstable steps, no one judges us for the failures. No one mocks us when we fall. We get up and try again.

As we get older and our physical legs become stronger, our emotional legs seem to grow weaker. We become self-conscious of our falling and failing. We quickly look around to see if anyone saw us. Eventually, we avoid circumstances that may show us in a bad light. If we try and fail, what will people think? We stop trying.

I am so grateful that my parents insisted that I get back to riding Target. I wasn't happy about it at the time, but I would have missed years and years of enjoyment if they hadn't pressed. But that's horseback riding.

What blessings and joys have we missed in our lives because we were afraid to look foolish? What new opportunities passed by us because we didn't want anyone to see us fall? I know, some may laugh at our bumps and bruises, but we have a God who brushes us off, heals our wounds, and encourages us to get back up and experience the rush of joy again! Try. Try again. Try again and again.

MEDITATIONS

Whom have I in heaven but you?

And earth has nothing I desire besides you. My flesh and my heart may fail, but God is the strength of my heart and my portion forever.

Psalm 73:25-26 (NIV)

So do not throw away your confidence; it will be richly rewarded. You need to persevere so that when you have done the will of God, you will receive what he has promised. For, "In just a little while, he who is coming will come and will not delay."

Hebrews 10:35-37 (NIV)

Consider it pure joy, my brothers and sisters, whenever you face trials of many kinds, because you know that the testing of your faith produces perseverance. Let perseverance finish its work so that you may be mature and complete, not lacking anything.

James 1:2-4 (NIV)

CHAPTER 13:
BLIND CALF

In all the years and all the calves, which was usually about eighty calves a year, I only remember one calf born with a disability. This calf was born without sight, and it was obvious just looking at her that something was wrong with her eyes. Where there was normally the beautiful deep brown eyes characteristic of jersey cows, instead there was a milking grey film, almost like cataracts over this young girl's eyes.

Although about eighty calves are born each year, the farmer does not keep all of them. First of all, about half of those calves will be little bulls, and a farm only needs a couple bulls to keep the whole herd "serviced" every year. But that still leaves about forty young heifers, and out of that lot, my dad would only keep about twenty to raise and eventually breed and ready to join the milking herd. And of course, my dad was always looking for the strongest to keep and would sell the rest at auction.

One would expect, then, that the little blind calf would not make the cut. I'm not sure why, but Dad kept the calf, raising it along with the other keepers of that season. It was amazing to watch her development and the response of the herd toward this new member of the community.

If you haven't gathered by some of the other stories presented here, there are many dangers and yes, literally pit falls, that exist on a dairy. There are riverbanks and ditches and fences and difficult terrain in which to navigate. A good pair of eyes seems essential to survive. A calf with no sight is at a significant disadvantage if left alone in this environment.

Of course, this calf was not alone. This calf was never alone. At first, she was with her fellow calves in the calf barn with a protected corral at one end. As the others roamed around their area, the calf stayed near and attempted to stay close and keep up with their movements. She was very attentive to the sound of their movements and seemed comfortable moving within the safety of their presence. As she grew larger in size, she also grew in confidence. No longer needing to be pressed up against another calf, she could travel back and forth across the corral independently and navigate herself back into the protection of the calf barn without event in the evening.

But a time was coming when she would have to be moved out of that confined and protected space with the others. No longer would she be safe in the 400 square yard corral that she had mapped in her head. She would have to move out into the open pastures below. No longer would she be protected by the smooth wood fences that encircled the corral, but she would move to a place with much wider boundaries and barbed wire fences.

I remember my dad being a bit worried about what would happen with the calf, now almost as large as her milking counterparts. What would happen when joined with the rest of the herd and the open fields?

We did not need to wait long. Almost immediately upon joining the herd, our nearly grown calf was not able to catch up with the movements of the herd. She was afraid, and the herd was too fast. The lead cows were moving out, and the calf got confused and started moving in the wrong direction. Very quickly, she found herself against the barbed wire fence and was pushing hard against it in panic. She cried out, and amazingly, the lead cows stopped their progress. They just stopped. They didn't turn, they didn't run back, and they didn't rescue the calf. They just stopped.

At some point, other cows moved closer to the calf and began to make lowing noises to coax her away from her dilemma and herd her back to the group. They didn't push or shove her, they didn't jump on the fence with her, they just got close enough so she could hear them. I've seen dogs herd cows, but I have never seen cows herd another cow. Somehow, they recognized the weakness in one of their members and accommodated her. From that point on, when the cows were on the move, the calf was placed in the middle of the group to ensure she was safe. And there were a few cows who seemed to be responsible for her, it wasn't the leaders, and it wasn't the entire herd... just a few.

Over time, the calf grew into adulthood and grew in confidence enough to walk independently most of the time. She was bred, had calves, and believe it or not, was able to learn the process of coming into the milking parlor and determining which stanchion was open for her entry (not easy, considering how many choices must be made, straight or to the right, first, second, or third stanchion. And the choice changes at every milking!). It was amazing to watch, not just her ability to learn, but the herd's ability to care for her.

It doesn't take much to get to a spiritual and community lesson from this story. In the herd there are leaders and the leaders have a plan and pace. The leaders are responsible to get the entire herd to follow. And although we all have weaknesses, there are some that are weaker than others.

In this scenario, the leaders identify that there is someone who needs help, so they stop their progress and wait. They wait for one of the herd to take responsibility. Those that follow take that signal and come alongside the weak one, and the weak one is returned to the herd. The weak one gets to borrow the confidence from the others until she has confidence of her own. She doesn't stay in a weakened state; she learns in the safety of the others and then becomes part of the community like all the others.

There are three points of view represented in this story: Leader, Stronger Members, and Weakened Member. When you are in the herd, everyone has a role to play. In a lifetime, we may find ourselves playing all of these roles at one time or another.

Maybe you are one of the leaders. Please take note of the obvious. Leaders Lead. Your job is to see forward, to navigate the path, to set the pace of the group, to recognize when there is trouble and respond by slowing the pace, if necessary. The leader does not do all the work, all the ministry, all the mentoring. I confess I have seen many a talented and devoted leader burn out, either by lacking adequate support of the membership, or refusing to relinquish any of the ministry responsibilities for fear of losing control. In the model of leadership employed by Jesus, He steps aside and lets others serve and minister.

Maybe you are one of the stronger members of the team. Your job is to come along side, catch the direction and pace of the leader and provide ministry and support for the one who has fallen behind. In the herd, there are no spectators. Every cow, to remain in the herd, must produce and reproduce.

Maybe you are the weakened one. In life, there are times and areas where every member may be the weak one. Your job is to recognize your weakness, recognize your need for help, ask for help, and then eventually accept it.

But contrary to popular practice, the weaker member is not a permanent position. At some point, victory over the weakness is an immediate opportunity to help another, to come along side as someone did for you, and move another from weakness to strength.

Call it whatever you want, there are many names for it: Community of believers, The Body of Christ, The Church, Community of faith... God's Herd! We need each other; we need to be in a place where we can serve the weakest among us so that we all become stronger. We were never intended to navigate the giant fields of life alone. The world is full of vast and scary spaces, surrounded by barbed fences, and full of those who cannot see clearly to navigate their way. Inside His herd, we all have a job to do. Just like those cows who took care of the blind calf, we are asked to care for others. There's another word for that, too: LOVE. Love One Another. The New Testaments repeats it over and over again. Love your leaders, love the stronger members, love those that are weak. Love One Another.

By this, the world will know us.

MEDITATIONS

A new command I give you:

Love one another. *As I have **love**d you, so you must **love one another***.

John 13:34

By this everyone will know that you are my disciples, if you **love one another***.*

John 13:35

Be devoted to **one another** *in* **love***. Honor* **one another** *above yourselves.*

Romans 12:10

Let no debt remain outstanding, except the continuing debt to **love one another***, for whoever* **love***s others has fulfilled the law.*

Romans 13:8

You, my brothers and sisters, were called to be free. But do not use your freedom to indulge the flesh; rather, serve **one another** *humbly in* **love***.*

Galatians 5:13

Be completely humble and gentle; be patient, bearing with **one another** *in* **love***.*

Ephesians 4:2

Now about your **love** *for* **one another** *we do not need to write to you, for you yourselves have been taught by God to* **love** *each other.*

1 Thessalonians 4:9

And let us consider how we may spur **one another** *on toward* **love** *and good deeds,*

Hebrews 10:24

Now that you have purified yourselves by obeying the truth so that you have sincere love for each other, love one another deeply, from the heart.

1 Peter 1:22

Finally, all of you, be like-minded, be sympathetic, **love one another**, *be compassionate and humble.*

1 Peter 3:8

For this is the message you heard from the beginning: We should **love one another**.

1 John 3:11

And this is his command: to believe in the name of his Son, Jesus Christ, and to **love one another** *as he commanded us.*

1 John 3:23

Dear friends, let us **love one another**, *for* **love** *comes from God. Everyone who* **loves** *has been born of God and knows God.*

1 John 4:7

*Dear friends, since God so **loved** us, we also ought to **love one another**.*

1 John 4:11

*No **one** has ever seen God; but if we **love one another**, God lives in us and his **love** is made complete in us.*

1 John 4:12

*And now, dear lady, I am not writing you a new command but **one** we have had from the beginning. I ask that we **love one another**.*

2 John 1:5

CHAPTER 14:
THE FASTEST ROUTE

We were not the only ones in our family with a horse or two. My grandfather was quite the horseman, and I never knew him to be without at least one horse in his possession. Grandpa also owned a dairy ranch about fifteen miles from ours, and on occasion, I would stay over and travel around his vast property on horseback.

I was older by this time and quite capable of catching and saddling his horse, Babe. Babe had an entirely different personality than our beloved Target, by the way. If you have ever owned dogs or cats, you know that animals have as many distinctive personalities as human beings. Same with horses.

Babe was easy to catch and, unlike Target, so willing to be saddled and ridden all over the trails Grandpa had carved out from his frequent horse riding on his ranch. And Babe was very fun to ride. She was fast and had a very even gait as soon as you got her out of her trot. You don't know the different speeds, or gaits, of a horse? There are basically four, and here's a little tutorial:

- the four-beat walk, which averages 4.0 mph
- the two-beat trot or jog at about 10 mph
- the canter or lope, a three-beat gait that is up to 15 mph
- the gallop, which averages 25-30 mph (although the fastest recorded is almost 44 mph)

Okay, the walk seems obvious. The horse walks. Easy. But the trot is interesting and depending on the horse, can be an internal organ juggling ordeal. My horse, Target, was a wonderful trot ride. Nice and smooth, easy to stay in the saddle, internal organs safe from bruising!

Babe was not a smooth ride when in her trot! I have ridden many horses over the course of my life, and no horse made it harder to stay in the saddle during a trot than Babe. To survive, I tried to get Babe either slower or faster than a trot as fast as I could. But, as rough a ride as her trot, she was as smooth as butter in her canter. And when she broke into her gallop—her dead-on run—she was amazing. It was exhilarating and so smooth it felt like you were gliding across the hills on air when she ran. I loved riding Babe fast.

And as I mentioned earlier, she loved to be ridden. She accepted the bit and saddle like they were treats. She sauntered around the trails of my grandfather's property and was very responsive to the signals I gave her to turn, go faster, go slower, stop. I could be out there riding for hours with no issue.

On one occasion, however, I completely underestimated HER enthusiasm to get back home.

I'm not sure what her issue was, and at first, there is no problem. I had been riding for hours, meandering, and admiring the beautiful grasses that swayed in the gentle breeze. But eventually, it was time to go home. I decided to forego the long winding path through the trees because I knew that would take more time than I wanted to spend. I was hungry and tired. I decided to take her up and over a couple of hills that would provide a much quicker return to the paddock. It wasn't the easiest path, but it was the shortest.

Not a problem. I squeezed her sides ever so slightly to signal her I was ready to pick up the pace as we progressed up the hill. Still no problem. Then we crested the hill and her paddock and tack area came into view, specifically HER view.

The only thing in my experience that comes close to what happened next is the first time I rode California Screamin' roller coaster at Disneyland. You know the one that goes from zero to 55 mph in 4.7 seconds? It takes your breath away, and on that day, Babe's acceleration toward her stall did the same to me!

Admittedly, Babe did not accelerate to 55 mph, but then, California Screamin' doesn't conclude its ride by running its passengers into a wooden roofline too short to clear! That's right, I was quickly headed for trouble, literally, and I knew it.

As hard as my arms could pull, they pulled. But Babe kept running. I panicked as Babe quickly closed the gap between pastoral bliss and sudden death. I thought about baling out to the side, but the chances of still getting severely injured by Babe's flying hooves was high. I held on and kept on pulling, and praying, and pulling.

Now you can imagine that my prayers were not the kind you hear in church or those lofty prayers one hears on movies. I was seconds away from disaster, so an "Oh Holy God our Father, Creator of the Universe" kind of prayer was not going to cut it. And it wasn't one of those quiet whispery hush prayers, so reverent and sweet. NO! My prayer was at the top of my lungs and went something like, "God, I'm going to die! Stop this horse!" "In Jesus Name" was implied! A screaming prayer and bloody hands on the reins… that's all I had. I'm surprised the reins didn't break in my hands or that my hands didn't break under the strains of the straps. Screaming prayer and bloody hands… that's all I had going for me.

Thankfully, and I do mean OH SO thankfully, blood and prayer were enough. At the last moment, as we lunged toward the roofline, I braced for impact and, while still holding tight to the useless reins, threw up my forearms in front of my face to protect against the imminent blow that was about to come. And then suddenly, she stopped. The inertia of our forward progress and her sudden brakes nearly through me over her head and into that roofline wall that I was so desperately trying to avoid. Miraculously, my forward progress was stopped by Babe's raised head, and in that moment, she turns around and just looks at me, as if to say, "Okay, we're home!"

It took me a while to finally catch my breath and unwind the reigns twisted and cutting into my hands. I sat in that saddle for several minutes, waiting for the remainder of my life to pass by me. Finally, I stepped hard and straight-legged with my left foot in its stirrup, swung my shaky right leg over, and dismounted.

Everything on my body was aching and tense, but I managed to take Babe's saddle and blanket off, brush her down (yes, I thought about leaving that part out, but it really is not good for the horse), and finally released her into the paddock, but not without a few words like, "You nearly killed me! What were you thinking?" There may have been other words... I cannot remember exactly.

Never again did I take the most direct path back to the paddock when riding Babe. There were safer, more level paths to take. There were paths that concealed the destination far better with turns and trees and other distractions, delaying her exuberance, and reducing the chance of me being maimed.

Lesson learned. Sometimes the most direct path is not the best. Of course, after returning Babe to her home, I got myself cleaned up and headed for my grandparents' house and inevitably the conversation about "How was your ride?" I felt a little foolish and ashamed telling my grandpa that I lost control of his horse, but there was no disguising the wounds on my hands, so the truth had to come out. As I related the events of the afternoon to him, he started to laugh out loud. "Oh yes, she gets very insistent coming over that hill! I don't bring her home that way, anymore!" Well, now you tell me!

In my own wisdom (and apparently Grandpa had tried it once, too), it feels right to take the shortest route, to just get home and get done. But shortest routes can be deceiving. Sure, it all looks good on paper, but there can be dangers of which I am unaware, factors I have not considered, results I have not anticipated or wanted.

I know I was lucky that day. I was blessed to return home mostly in one piece, rather than in an emergency room or worse. But, I am still an impatient rider, an impatient navigator of my own life. I'm always looking for the shortest route, wondering and frustrated at the delays and detours that inevitably come my way. I jump to the conclusion that it is evil that blocks my progress, rather than a loving hand of God and His wisdom who knows the things I do not.

Think about the paths of all who have walked this life before us. Those that remained faithful as life dealt them delays in God's promises, thwarted dreams and visions, and blockades to callings and destinations. When you peruse scripture, it is difficult not to notice that the "long way" seems to be God's way. Spiritual growth is rarely the sprint that Babe took that day.

Next time you are getting impatient with your own life's progress, remember Babe. Have faith that God sees things on your path that you cannot see. Have faith that He will get you home in His way and it is the best way. Have faith, protect your head and heart, and take the long way home!

MEDITATIONS

Now faith is confidence in what we hope for and assurance about what we do not see. This is what the ancients were commended for.

By faith we understand that the universe was formed at God's command, so that what is seen was not made out of what was visible.

By faith Abel brought God a better offering than Cain did. By faith he was commended as righteous, when God spoke well of his offerings. And by faith Abel still speaks, even though he is dead.

By faith Enoch was taken from this life, so that he did not experience death: "He could not be found, because God had taken him away." For before he was taken, he was commended as one who pleased God. And without faith it is impossible to please God, because anyone who comes to him must believe that he exists and that he rewards those who earnestly seek him.

By faith Noah, when warned about things not yet seen, in holy fear built an ark to save his family. By his faith he condemned the world and became heir of the righteousness that is in keeping with faith.

By faith Abraham, when called to go to a place he would later receive as his inheritance, obeyed and went, even though he did not know where he was going. By faith he made his home in the promised land like a stranger in a foreign country; he lived in tents, as did Isaac and Jacob, who were heirs with him of the same promise. For he was looking forward to the city with foundations, whose architect and builder is God. And by faith even Sarah, who was past childbearing age, was enabled to bear children because she considered him faithful who had made the promise. And so from this one man, and he as good as dead, came descendants as numerous as the stars in the sky and as countless as the sand on the seashore.

All these people were still living by faith when they died. They did not receive the things promised; they only saw them and welcomed them from a distance, admitting that they were foreigners and strangers on earth. People who say such things show that they are looking for a country of their own. If they had been thinking of the country they had left, they would have had opportunity to return. Instead, they were longing for a better country—a heavenly one. Therefore God is not ashamed to be called their God, for he has prepared a city for them.

By faith Abraham, when God tested him, offered Isaac as a sacrifice. He who had embraced the promises was about to sacrifice his one and only son, even though God had said to him, "It is through Isaac that your offspring will be reckoned." Abraham reasoned that God could even raise the dead, and so in a manner of speaking he did receive Isaac back from death.

By faith Isaac blessed Jacob and Esau in regard to their future.

By faith Jacob, when he was dying, blessed each of Joseph's sons, and worshiped as he leaned on the top of his staff.

By faith Joseph, when his end was near, spoke about the exodus of the Israelites from Egypt and gave instructions concerning the burial of his bones.

By faith Moses' parents hid him for three months after he was born, because they saw he was no ordinary child, and they were not afraid of the king's edict.

By faith Moses, when he had grown up, refused to be known as the son of Pharaoh's daughter. He chose to be mistreated along with the people of God rather than to enjoy the fleeting pleasures of sin. He regarded disgrace for the sake of Christ as of greater value than the treasures of Egypt, because he was looking ahead to his reward. By faith he left Egypt, not fearing the king's anger; he persevered because he saw him who is invisible. By faith he kept the Passover and the application of blood, so that the destroyer of the firstborn would not touch the firstborn of Israel.

By faith the people passed through the Red Sea as on dry land; but when the Egyptians tried to do so, they were drowned.

By faith the walls of Jericho fell, after the army had marched around them for seven days.

By faith the prostitute Rahab, because she welcomed the spies, was not killed with those who were disobedient.

And what more shall I say? I do not have time to tell about Gideon, Barak, Samson and Jephthah, about David and Samuel and the prophets, who through faith conquered kingdoms, administered justice, and gained what was promised; who shut the mouths of lions, quenched the fury of the flames, and escaped the edge of the sword; whose weakness was turned to strength; and who became powerful in battle and routed foreign armies. Women received back their dead, raised to life again. There were others who were tortured, refusing to be released so that they might gain an even better resurrection. Some faced jeers and flogging, and even chains and imprisonment. They were put to death by stoning; they were sawed in two; they were killed by the sword. They went about in sheepskins and goatskins, destitute, persecuted and mistreated—the world was not worthy of them. They wandered in deserts and mountains, living in caves and in holes in the ground.

These were all commended for their faith, yet none of them received what had been promised, since God had planned something better for us so that only together with us would they be made perfect.

Hebrews 11 (NIV)

CHAPTER 15:
SIDNEY'S NIGHT OUT

Although we obviously had many animals around while growing up, but most were not considered pets. We did, however, have a couple of horses over the years, our collie dog cleverly named Lassie, a couple of rabbits (indeed, a phase of mine) and one cat, the only pet that was allowed inside the house. Pets had names, the other animals did not.

Sidney was really my sister Diane's cat. His full name was Sidney George Crockett, the first. He was your typical tabby, mostly black, and full of self-serving and regal attitude. He liked being petted unless he didn't want to be petted. He was overfed and overindulged in all ways. We met his expectations of being let in when he desired, being let out when he demanded, and keeping the bowl full of food at all times. He had us well-trained. He was ridiculous.

One funny habit he developed over the years was to prowl around all night, be let in first thing in the morning, and then meander his way into the kitchen to stand in front of the refrigerator as a sign that the master was ready for breakfast. His food wasn't even stored in the refrigerator, so I am not sure why that became his habit, but again, we all complied with his signaled wishes every morning.

All of this is needed background for an event that occurred one September when I was sixteen, and my sisters were in college. My mom and dad's twenty-fifth wedding anniversary was approaching, and the parents and daughters had prepared for a big shindig at the house. There was a beautiful, tiered cake ordered, but mom and the sisters did most of the food preparation. We were expecting at least 150 friends and family, and the party was going to go on for hours, people dropping in and out as they wished.

There was also a significant amount of celebratory alcohol on the menu, including champagne and a keg full of beer. My parents were by no means partier kind of people, so the keg purchase was a very unusual provision.

The day arrived and was a huge success. People came, ate a little, drank a little, and congratulated my parents on their long-standing marriage. People from their childhood drove over 100 miles to share in the festivities. Family from all over arrived, reminisced, and shared jokes and stories until the late evening.

Eventually, the good wishers departed, and don't forget, Dad had to go down to the barn to milk cows. There is no resting from this cycle, I promise, not even for a 25th wedding anniversary.

After the cows were milked and the bulk of the party cleanup was completed at the house, Dad began to wonder what to do with the keg that still stood in the middle of the yard. The problem was the keg still had lots of beer remaining, as most people were drinking champagne during the party. We lived amongst a small and overly informed community, so everyone within a twenty mile radius would know about the party. Dad hesitated to leave the keg as it was, for fear of neighbor kids sneaking onto the property and emptying its contents while we slept. Not wanting to contribute to anyone else's mayhem or being held liable for anything resulting from that keg, Dad decided to empty it out into the yard. That seemed the best course of action at the time.

Of course, the next morning, all of us were exhausted from the previous day's activities. We sat down to breakfast, and at some point, someone asked about Sidney and his whereabouts. Dad got up from the table and went to the back door to let in the cat, as was customary. Dad opened the door (which was not within sight of the kitchen) and we could hear Dad chuckling. We waited and wondered what was so funny. We waited and all looked toward the kitchen door for the grand entrance of the prince of the kingdom. We waited. We waited some more, wondering what was taking Sidney so long, and we could still hear Dad laughing.

And there he was. Sidney, walking at quite a slow pace, and not walking in a straight line. Bobbing and weaving, Sidney finally managed to cross the kitchen threshold and navigate his way to his customary place in front of the refrigerator. He paused and finally, with great effort, he managed to turn and face the refrigerator. He paused again, his head bobbed forward, then back, and then... plunk! He abruptly fell face forward into the refrigerator and remained in a sort of Tower of Pisa position and stayed there! Yep, Sidney was drunk.

It did not take long to figure out that the keg that was poured out onto the lawn was discovered by the cat and he had indulged himself the whole night long. Sidney had been on a bender!

Although we were all laughing, the voice I remember is my mom's. She could not stop laughing. Incredible that the cat was drunk. In fact, he really was the only one who got drunk from the celebration, everyone else managed to be well-behaved. But not Sidney.

It took Sidney quite some time to recover from his ordeal, mainly sleeping it off all day and night, and most of the next day. This story has become lore in my family... "you remember the time Sidney got drunk and fell into the fridge?" There's no spiritual lesson of which I am aware on this one, just a great story and memory to retell. Welcome to the family!

CHAPTER 16:
IRRIGATION PIPE

I have said it before, and I'll say it again. Farming is all about rhythm. On a ranch, there is rhythm everywhere, and one of the most nostalgic rhythms for me is the sound of the irrigation system doing its job, watering the fields in the heat of summer. It resembles a heartbeat, and every time I hear it, I can almost feel the open air and smell the luscious grass beneath.

Keeping 200 acres of grass watered during the summer is not like your sprinklers at home. Irrigation of a field does not involve a hose with a sprinkler head at the end. Instead, it is accomplished by lengths of large, heavy pipe about fifteen feet long. With 200 acres, you cannot water all of the fields at the same time, so it requires a system, a plan, a strategy. Here's how it worked at our place.

Irrigation pipe is not one pipe, but many lengths of pipe hooked together with sprinklers on each pipe. Every pipe has a heavy metal hook on one end and a slot on the other.

The lengths of pipe are laid out in one long line across the end of a field, connected by the alternating hooks and slots, and would remain in this location for several days, depending on the weather.

Once the watering was sufficient for its coverage, the line of pipe would be moved further down the field. Over the course of a couple of weeks, the entire field would be watered, and the process would either start again, or the pipes would be moved to another field by trailer where the same process would be utilized.

Normally there were five of us available to move pipe, so based on that number, we could move four lengths of pipe represented by an → below. The pointed end of the arrow represents the hooked end, whereas the other end has a slot. The pipes are held together as the hook of one pipe is slid into the slot of the previous pipe and pulled tight.

Chapter 16: Irrigation Pipe

The group would disconnect pipes at the end of the row from their current location. Each person would pick up an end of a pipe, and walk together in a line, about 30 feet, and one by one, hook their pipe to a new connector that had previously been prepared by my dad. The simple version of this process is, after the first four pipes were all connected, the group would return to the original line of pipes and repeat the process, four pipes at a time, back and forth, until the entire line was relocated.

This is the simplified version of the explanation. Now for the detail and importance of keeping the right rhythm.

Every pipe has two people responsible for it, one at each end. Disconnecting the pipes requires a person (#1) on the "open end" of the line of pipes to LIFT up their end and PUSH the pipe toward the connected end of the pipe. This will RELEASE the hook of the disconnecting pipe from the groove or slot of the next pipe. Once the hook and slot are separated, the other person (#2) LIFT up their end of the first pipe by the hook with their left hand and SLIDE it away from the other pipe. THEN, #2 becomes the new #1 and performs the same push and release motion on the pipe to their right. Down the line it goes, LIFT, PUSH, RELEASE, LIFT, SLIDE...LIFT, PUSH, RELEASE, LIFT, SLIDE until there are four released pipes.

Now, all five people bend down and pick up their pipes, three people in the middle all have ends of two pipes, the first and last person only hold one end. Then all five walk the four lengths of pipe forward thirty feet and restart the connecting process in the new location.

Although there is a rhythm in the disconnecting and moving of the pipes, the real skill comes in the reconnecting in the new location. In this case, rhythm, the right rhythm, becomes a necessity. If you are not in rhythm with the rest of the folks on the crew, the results can be quite painful! Fingers need to be out of the way when someone pushes on the pipe!

It stands to reason that the reconnecting process is just a reversal of the disconnecting on the previous row, right?

Right. This time, it is the person on the far right of the walking line that prepares the pipe to be reconnected. The first person only has one pipe in their left hand and sets the pipe end into the pipe to his right, holding it by the hook.

Now here is the problem. Unlike small pipes, the person does not have enough strength or leverage from his end to fully connect the pipes by themselves, but rather, can only get the two connections a few centimeters in. Once set, the person on their left shoves the pipe from their end to the right, clearing the hook passed the open slot of the next pipe, and then, with some force, pulls the pipe back in the opposite direction. When this happens, the hook will now slide firmly into the slot and the connection between the two pipes will be secure. If the person on the hook end of the pipe neglects to let go at just the right time, one of two things can happen.

First, if the person lets go of the tenuous connection between the two pipes too soon, the hook may slide off and miss the connection of the slot when it is pulled back. The two pipes will disconnect, and the setting of the pipe will have to be restarted. Regardless, losing the rhythm slows the whole process down, so everyone is impacted by a miss. Remember, everyone else is still holding heavy pipes waiting for their turn.

Second, and much worse, if the person does not let go soon enough, the fingers will remain holding on to the hook while it is sliding into the slot. Let me tell you, you only

Farmer God

make this mistake once. These are extremely heavy pipes, and in a war between galvanized metal pipe and flesh and bone, the pipe will always win! There is a rhythm: slide, set, pull, connect. Miscalculate the timing of the rhythm, and not only is everyone else on the crew impacted, but the one who lost the rhythm may lose more than that. At the very least, they will feel that miss for days and days, and may not be able to tie their shoes, eat with a fork, or brush their teeth without a tremendous amount of pain and effort.

Moving an irrigation pipe, even with five people, was still an arduous and lengthy process. One of our fields may have had as many as forty lengths of pipe that needed to be moved every few days. Doing the math, that disconnecting and reconnecting process would have to occur ten times. Even under the best of circumstances, the process takes at least an hour. Can you imagine if only four people showed up at the field one day? Now only three pipes can be moved at a time, but the impact becomes exponential. Now instead of moving forty lengths of pipe in an hour, it will take about an hour and a half! And with only three people? They can carry only two pipes at a time, but it is not just double the original time amount of one hour, but more like triple! You see, every time the pipes are set, the team, however big or small it is, has to walk back to the original line thirty feet away to disconnect the previous line of pipes and walk another thirty feet to the new line.

Think how long this process would take if only one person attempted to move the irrigation pipes. It might take

132

all day because the leverage realized with a team is now lost.

Tell me you don't get the spiritual lesson of this story. It is not that the efforts of one becoming two doubles the results, it's that it MORE than doubles the results. And with each added to the crew, the efficiencies gained are more than the number added. Truly, if we had forty-one people on the crew to move forty lengths of pipe, the job could be done in a matter of a few minutes, and there would be no need to walk back thirty feet for another set of pipes!

As a body of believers, we truly are more than the sum of our parts. Every person involved in a task or project needs to function within and for the rest of the team. There is a rhythm in the Kingdom, just like there is a rhythm in moving irrigation pipe. Together, we can accomplish so much more!

MEDITATIONS

*The LORD God said, "It is **not** good for the man to be **alone**. I will make a helper suitable for him.*

Genesis 2:18

The LORD said to Moses: "Bring me seventy of Israel's elders who are known to you as leaders and officials among the people. Have them come to the tent of meeting, that they may stand there with you. I will come down and speak with you there, and I will take some of the power of the Spirit that is on you and put it on them. They will share the burden of the people with you so that you will not have to carry it alone.

Numbers 11:16-17 (NIV)

Two are better than one, because they have a good return for their labor: If either of them falls down, one can help the other up.

Ecclesiastes 4:9-10 (NIV)

*From him the whole body, joined and held **together** by every supporting ligament, grows and builds itself up in love, as each part does its **work**.*

Ephesians 4:16

CHAPTER 17:
THE WOOL BAG

When you live on a dairy ranch outside a small town, you end up with friends who also live in the country or at least have family living on farms. And with those relationships, I ended up with experiences and lessons on their properties as well as my own.

I recently reconnected with one of those friends, Kay, who reminded me of an experience that occurred on her "Poppy's" sheep ranch.

Let's make it clear. Sheep are not cows. It's true that all those scriptures referring to people being like sheep could, in some regard, just as easily render the same lesson if you compare us to cows. We are easily lost, a little limited in our ability to get ourselves out of trouble, and generally safest following the rest of the flock or herd.

But in most other ways, the similarities are few and far between. Raising sheep is very different from raising cows.

You can tell the minute you step onto a sheep ranch that you are not on a dairy farm anymore!

I spent many summers hanging out with Kay at her house "in town:" listening to music, riding bikes in her neighborhood, and playing in the field just below her family's property. But one day, I was invited to tag along to Kay's grandpa Poppy's sheep ranch. It sounded fun!

What I had not realized was that the tag along invitation was for help on the ranch. Today was sheep shearing day, and they needed extra hands to harvest the wool.

Now before you get the idea that wool is like those fluffy white clouds of wonderful puff and warmth that you are probably used to, please know, wool does not start off that way. I know, cute pictures of sheep standing in the field, all cute and curly… it's so adorable! Who wouldn't want to help collect all that fluffy, cuddly stuff?

I knew a little about sheep. Our next-door neighbors ran sheep on their property. I remember the transformation that occurs after the shearing has been completed, where the lambs go from big balls of adorableness, to short shorn and naked looking, but still remain adorable animals romping on the hillside! After the shearing, the lambs all looked so fresh and energetic, and frankly, cooler as the days got warmer and longer.

I also appreciated sheep poop. Really? Really! Wait for a second, I'll get to it.

You see, when you have spent the greater part of your childhood shoveling cow poop in all seasons, including winter when many of the cows were experiencing very loose poop because of the very wet grass on muddy fields, you can really appreciate the compact and let's just say it, solid little deposits that sheep make.

Once a season, it was my job to collect and remove all the sheep deposits from the picnic area around the lake that was behind my house. This amazing property owned by our neighbors was the best place to swim, water ski, barbeque, and of course, have the greatest Fourth of July picnic to which all the neighbors came. In preparation for all that activity, the sheep were moved further up the hillside, and their poop cleaned up for the summer season. So yes, when it is your job to pick up the poop, and you are used to cow poop, sheep poop is just so much more… convenient (there is more than just a little coincidence that I started this project talking about poop, and now ending with more).

Back to Poppy's ranch. We arrived, and I was very excited to see what the day had in store for us. We were informed that we would get to help in the shearing! I'm sure, in my mind, I thought that I was going to learn how to shear sheep. Boy, was I wrong!

As we approached the shearing area, it was impossible not to notice a very strange sight. Hanging from very high wooden platforms were long burlap sacks… the wool bags.

Don't be distracted by the foreground and all the shearing activity there. Look beyond the shearer to the bag that is hanging from the platform behind him. THAT is a wool bag and it can hold up to 250 pounds of packed down wool. How does the wool get packed down? After the shearer completes his job, the wool is thrown up to someone on the platform who then throws it down into the bottom of the bag, where, unfortunately for me, a person with no other skills but walking around in a very small circle is waiting!

We walked over to see the very high platform, and a bag, not yet hung, laying on the ground. And so, it began. Kay went first, because of course, she had done this before. I have no memory of her turn, other than it happened. My only memories are my personal experiences. A fresh and empty wool bag was laying on the shear floor, sides nicely coiled up with a little empty space in the middle. I was asked to step into the open space of the bag, and then the coiled-up sides were lifted up and around me, until the top of the bag was hooked to the platform seven or eight feet above.

Now, picture it. A small girl standing in the bottom of a brown, stinky, hot, burlap bag, with little to no visibility, little light, and frankly, not much air. A sheep is shorn and suddenly a bunch of wool comes plummeting down from the top of the bag right onto my head. Remember those visions of fluffy white clouds from earlier? Gone! What comes pelting down (pun intended) is a giant and heavy mass of oily, smelly, dirty, sheep wool that is more grey than white. Of course, the tendency at first is to look up to the only lighted place, which is the hole eight feet above. If your timing is off, that mass of stinky fuzz lands right on your face and whatever is lurking among the wool fibers ends up in your nose and yes, mouth.

Adding to that unpleasantness is the fact that in most cases, the wool is NOT just wool, but everything that has hijacked itself onto the wool in the lamb's world, like ends of briars, pieces of wood, and yes, that ever-present substance on animal farms, POOP!

In the midst of this onslaught of nastiness, my job was to get the wool under my feet and then walk around in a three foot circle and pound it down flat, in preparation for the next wool shower, which by the way, was coming down every two or three minutes (more rhythms of a ranch). It was hot and exhausting work. You might think, "It's just walking around," but it was not that. I'm always up for a nice little stroll, but as the bag filled, the job got harder and harder to keep the compression because the floor was getting softer and softer. The taller the stack of wool grew, the harder the job became.

And there is really no way out of this situation, except to keep on walking, trying to avoid the wool hitting your face, and keeping the wool patted down across the circumference of the bag, all while waiting for the next wool bundle. And all the while, the guy at the top is yelling down warnings of when the next wool will be dropped, "Here it comes", and pointing out places that need my attention.

As I walked and walked, sweating, and covered with lanolin, the stack grew taller and taller and I got closer and closer to the fresh air at the top of the bag. Let me tell you, that fresh air was quite an incentive. On my way up, I occasionally got a whiff of it or a feel of it, so I kept on walking around in those tight little circles.

Eventually, since I was still alive, I made it to the top and was pulled up and out of the bag and onto the platform. Then, the bag top was sewn together and dropped from its holding pegs. The tower of burlap and wool fell to the shearing floor and its girth maneuvered to the awaiting scales to measure. I have no idea how close my bags were to the coveted 250 pounds, but the heaviest bag of the day definitely went to Kay, and she was definitely deserving of the resulting bragging rights. Believe me, the heaviest bag is a thing!

Regardless of the winner, all of us lucky enough to have been a wool compressor basically looked the same. Every inch of skin, hair, and clothes were a dark and greasy grey color. We were only recognizable by body shape. All other distinguishing characteristics were erased with layers of lanolin, sweat, and yes, poop.

I can assure you that this process is greatly modernized and automated now. Most farmers have machines that pound down the wool like a giant trash compactor (do people even have those anymore?) into a neat bale, which is put on a conveyor belt for storage and shipment. But automation of this kind rarely results in a spiritual lesson!

Ever feel like your life is basically at the bottom of a stinky bag and you have no way to see, get out, or even breathe? If you are part of the human race, you have probably experienced this at one time or another. Sometimes, this comes to us as a very, long season of walking in circles without vision or seemingly progress, and it just seems it will never end.

These times are inevitable! No matter who we are, where we've been, and where we come from, there is no way to navigate life without experiencing seasons of this kind. And what is the solution?

You may have guessed it, but here it is. Keep on walking!

Can you imagine if Kay or I had decided to give up and just slump ourselves down on the miniscule pile of wool beneath our feet? All that heavy wool falling from the bag opening, from the sky, would just pile up, and eventually, we would be buried in wool. Not very productive and possibly dangerous. So, we just kept on walking, and as we walked, the very thing that was falling down on us became the rising foundation under our feet. Hear this in a different way: Every time we are able to overcome the trials that come down on us, that trial becomes part of the foundation that lifts us up.

The more we walked, the higher we were positioned in the bag. Eventually, we reached the top of the bag and could escape. That's right! That's life!

When going through tough times, when everything seems to be coming down on me, it is easy to be deceived into thinking it will bury me, that it is only happening to me. It is tempting to think I cannot overcome it because the solution is not readily available, that clean air and rest will never come. My mind and heart cannot fathom the reality of being at the top of the heap.

But there are folks at the top of the bag that are ready to

pull us out, if only we will endure, if we just keep on walking on the very troubles that plague our lives. Overcoming is like that bag. Overcoming is learning to walk in the midst of the trouble and to KNOW that with each tiny step is also a tiny victory that brings us closer to the top. Not giving up is a victory in itself.

You see, when troubles and trials come raining down on wool bag life, I think there must be a fast and easy escape. If I have enough faith, if I'm strong enough or spiritual enough, I should just be able to climb out of the bag, but life doesn't always work that way. Walking in faith doesn't always work that way. We cannot strong arm our way out of the bag!

To keep walking, even when you can't see the top... that is faith. To keep walking, even when more and more trials fall on your head... that is faith. To keep walking, even when you are not sure what the outcome will be at the end... that is faith. And God asks us to walk by it! Dark, hot, sweaty, smelly, poopy walking in circles is the NORM of faith, not the exception.

Thankfully, for all believers, although we walk by faith alone, we do not walk alone in our faith. So many have walked before, and many walk with us now. \One of the greatest motivations for me that day in the wool bag was to know Kay had survived the experience. She was one of the people at the top of the bag yelling down warnings, but also encouragement.

Okay, sure, each of us must walk in our own individual wool bag, but the result or outcome is the same. Because each of us have a God who knows what it's like to walk in this way. And He is there, at the top of the platform, keeping us safe, sending encouragements and corrections with each step, waiting to lift us up into His glorious fresh air!

And what about the fluffy white stuff we know as wool? After much cleaning and combing, it gets transformed into for all kinds of wonderful and useful things. But now, you know it doesn't start that way, and of course, neither do we! Yes, a spiritual lesson can also be found at the bottom of a wool bag!

MEDITATIONS

*I have been crucified with Christ and I no longer **live**, but Christ **live**s in me. The life I now **live** in the body, I **live by faith** in the Son of God, who loved me and gave himself for me.*

Galatians 2:20

We sent Timothy, who is our brother and co-worker in God's service in spreading the gospel of Christ, to strengthen and encourage you in your faith, so that no one would be unsettled by these trials. For you know quite well that we are destined for them. In fact, when we were with you, we kept telling you that we would be persecuted. And it turned out that way, as you well know.

We live by faith, not by sight.

1 Thessalonians 3:2-4

*Consider it pure joy, my brothers and sisters, whenever you face **trials** of many kinds, because you know that the testing of your faith produces perseverance. Let perseverance finish its work so that you may be mature and complete, not lacking anything.*

James 1:2-4

Blessed is the one who perseveres under trial because, having stood the test, that person will receive the crown of life that the Lord has promised to those who love him.

James 1:12

In all this you greatly rejoice, though now for a little while you may have had to suffer grief in all kinds of **trials**.

1 Peter 1:6

if this is so, then the Lord knows how to rescue the godly from **trials** *and to hold the unrighteous for punishment on the day of judgment.*

2 Peter 2:9

CHAPTER 18:
LAKE COQUILLE

Never heard of it? Not surprising. The fact of the matter is, no one from my little town of Coquille have ever heard of it, either. It doesn't really exist. But, for at least one visitor to our picturesque valley, it did.

You see, things do not always appear as they really are. In certain times and seasons, one can get an impression that forms a belief or assumption that is just simply inaccurate. It's human nature to form an opinion or belief on very little information. Such was the case for one gentleman who visited our area.

I'm not sure what month it was, but it was certainly near the end of the rainy season. Now, it's true: it rains a lot in the Pacific Northwest, so proclaiming we had a rainy season is relative. People visiting from dryer climates would probably guess that our rainy season lasts eleven months of the year, and in many cases, the natives probably feel the same! In truth, it gets really rainy between October and February. I get it, that's almost half the year, but if you are a stranger from out of town and you arrive in January after months and months of heavy rain, you will see the most beautiful body of water covering the valley and bordered by the surrounding green hills. It's quite lovely, albeit temporary.

One such visitor could not understand why our community had not taken more economic advantage of such a beautiful lake. He was one of those city slickers, and I'm sure he thought we were a bunch of uneducated bumpkins. He began to regale my dad with all the possibilities that were being missed. After all, someone could build cabins along the edge of the lake, rent out ski boats and fishing boats. What a vacation paradise this would be in the summer months, and what a financial boon it would be to a struggling community!

"Ah, yes," my dad replied, "there's just one problem with your plan! This amazing lake won't be here in the summer! It's not a lake. That area is a bunch of fields that are currently flooded from the winter and spring rains!"

The visitor could not believe it. In fact, he didn't believe it. Knowing Dad, he might just be pulling his leg. It had to be a lake, it was perfect and huge. No way could that just be fields.

Finally, my dad helped him with his disbelief. From the vantage of our house and looking slightly off to the right, one could just see the orderly tops of fence posts descending into the water. The visitor was convinced.

It would be years later that the same visitor came and saw the "lake" in the summer, which of course was indeed fields, fence posts, and cows grazing on the luscious grass of the season. We often referred to the valley as Lake Coquille as an inside joke, or for the unfortunate and uninformed out of towners.

And here is the problem with human nature. We draw conclusions and develop beliefs on insufficient information. We judge not only places, but more impactfully, we judge people. We glimpse only the tiniest of details about a person and their life, and our minds fill in all the gaps. We see slivers of a person's appearance or behavior, and we fool ourselves into believing we have sight of the whole pie.

When we see a person who seems so "put together" with the right clothes and the best shoes, drives a nice car and lives in a nice home, we assume things. We might assume their life is without struggle or hardship, we might guess that their personal and professional life is perfect and therefore, the person is completely fulfilled and happy.

What we are really seeing is a Lake Coquille in someone else's life. We see the outward appearance in a certain moment or season, and mistakenly believe we know what is going on the rest of the year. We see the surface and its beauty, never bothering to notice the fence posts and barbed wire underneath, the pain of struggle and sadness that lies below what we see.

And just like our out-of-town visitor, we need to look more closely. We need to turn our attention to the details with compassion and understanding. We need to borrow the eyes and insight of our loving Father, who sees all our fence posts and barbed wire, our experiences and disappointments, and still loves us without limit.

MEDITATIONS

Be merciful, just as your Father is merciful.

"Do not judge, and you will not be judged. Do not condemn, and you will not be condemned. Forgive, and you will be forgiven. Give, and it will be given to you. A good measure, pressed down, shaken together and running over, will be poured into your lap. For with the measure you use, it will be measured to you."

Luke 6:36-38 (NIV)

In the same way, the Spirit helps us in our weakness. We do not know what we ought to pray for, but the Spirit himself intercedes for us through wordless groans. And he who searches our hearts knows the mind of the Spirit, because the Spirit intercedes for God's people in accordance with the will of God.

And we know that in all things God works for the good of those who love him, who[a] have been called according to his purpose.

Romans 8:26-28 (NIV)

These are the things God has revealed to us by his Spirit.

The Spirit searches all things, even the deep things of God. For who knows a person's thoughts except their own spirit within them? In the same way no one knows the thoughts of God except the Spirit of God. What we have received is not the spirit of the world, but the Spirit who is from God, so that we may understand what God has freely given us.

1 Corinthians 2:10-12 (NIV)

Printed in the USA
CPSIA information can be obtained
at www.ICGtesting.com
LVHW050754160923
756757LV00030B/198